Flavorful Wild Game

A Cooking Adventure in Wild Game and Desserts

By

Valerie Morris

Recipes Edited by:

Margi Hemingway

Smith & Hemingway Associates

Cover Photo by:

Lynn Barton

Barton Photography

Flavorful Wild Game

Copyright © 2002
ISBN: 9-780972-199803
Library of Congress: 2001086782

For additional copies, see order form on the last page.

Printed in the United States of America

STARR ★ TOOF

670 South Cooper Street
Memphis, TN 38104

Dedicated to the people who consistently inspired me, loved me, challenged me, believed in me and cared for me ...

My Father ...
William H. Diener

My Culinary Mentors ...
Chef Ernest Prokos & Chef Bill Barum

Introduction

This book's personality evolved from my fortunate opportunities to travel and live in exciting places around the world. I have experienced the wonders of multi-cultural living on a first hand basis in over thirty countries. One thing that is consistent in any country is that most men and many women love to hunt. But, many hunters bring their game home for someone else to prepare, for they may love the hunt but not the cooking. Important to those who love to eat, game has a wonderful and distinct taste. My insight is a result of travel and diverse nationalities that have given me the knowledge to blend flavors from all over the world to make wild game as flavorful as possible.

This cookbook is a blend of flavors from North to South, East to West and around the world. As a chef, who loves wild game, but finds the strong game flavor sometimes overpowering, you will find these recipes full of flavor and easy to prepare. The desserts are some of my personal favorites to accent game menus. I have personally developed, tested and served all these recipes from dinner parties for eight to buffets for hundreds. Many of these recipes evolved from conversations with hunters, other wild game cooks and my personal love to experiment and share with my friends.

I hope you find these recipes as enjoyable ... and Flavorful as I do!

Chef Valerie

About Wild Game

Wild game varies from region to region, even in the same country. Also, weather conditions and local food supply for the game can affect the flavor and texture of the meat. All game has a wonderful and distinct taste, though properly dressing the meat in the field can be the key to fresh flavor.

If you are buying game, you can almost always be sure that it was farm-raised which will eliminate many of the concerns about age, flavor and texture. Ask your local butcher or meat market about a farm-raised game source. Some of the most readily available farm-raised game includes: rabbit, venison, emu, antelope, quail, elk, ostrich, rattlesnake and boar.

If you are a hunter, find a reputable processor to butcher your game properly. Be sure that all possible fat is removed from the meat, as this fat causes a lot of the "gaminess" and strong flavor that can permeate the meat. If you are grinding game for burgers, meatloaves or chilies, be sure to substitute some beef or pork suet for the game fat. At least a small amount of fat is essential for juicy burgers and moist meatloaves.

Always wash game thoroughly, even if it has been dressed and frozen. If frozen, it is best to let it thaw in the refrigerator.

The recipes in this book will explain the techniques for seasoning and preparation of each kind of game. Substitutions are always an option. If the recipe calls for elk, you can use venison ... be creative and don't be afraid to let your imagination run wild!

If you have questions about the legality of wild game and hunting in your area, please contact your local state conservation and wildlife management department. They can provide you with game season dates, limits on each type of game and licensing requirements.

Happy Hunting ... or shopping ... and Bon Appétit!

About the Author

Born in Brazil and raised in North Carolina, Chef Valerie Morris now calls Memphis, Tennessee home. She is an avid wild game cook, and for the past seven years has coordinated and prepared the Mayor's Annual Wild Game Dinner, a benefit for Opera Memphis. This is one event that all Memphis hunters, politicians and gourmands look forward to each January. Patrons get their chance to sample all kinds of exotic game—from rattlesnake to black bear, from kangaroo to beaver—all presented in imaginative recipes by a chef who knows how to bring out the unique flavor of each variety of wild game.

Chef Morris' formal culinary training came from Le Cordon Bleu l'Art Culinaire in Paris, France. She has won many awards and citations for her culinary expertise—in both desserts and wild game. Morris was the first female chef to be named Chef of the Year by the Greater Memphis Chapter of the American Culinary Federation, and she has recently been awarded the Millennium Chef International Award of Excellence, given to America's top 100 chefs, by the International Restaurant & Hospitality Bureau. Chef Morris has cooked at the renowned James Beard House in New York and continues to work as a professional chef and culinary educator. She is a member of the Memphis bailli of La Confrérie de la Chaîne des Rôtisseurs and is on the Board of Directors of the Memphis Chapter of the American Culinary Federation. Chef Morris conducts numerous cooking classes and demonstrations and has appeared on television cooking segments. Because she believes it is important to give back to the community, she is an active volunteer in helping raise funds for countless nonprofit and civic organizations—St. Jude's Foundation, Ducks Unlimited, American Heart Association, United Cerebral Palsy, Make-A-Wish Foundation, Ballet Memphis—just to name a few. The founder of River Terrace restaurant in Memphis, Chef Morris is currently the Director of Mid-South Culinary Arts and is a culinary consultant to Lifestyle Ventures and Equestria Restaurant, in Germantown, Tennessee.

Chef Morris has traveled throughout the world to over 30 countries, which is reflected in her culinary style and sense of flavors. In her spare time, she enjoys entertaining friends and family.

Table of Contents

Game Hors d'Oeuvres

Artichoke and Quail Dip

Makes 12 servings

2	14-ounce cans artichoke hearts, drained and chopped	¼	teaspoon garlic powder
1	cup quail meat, skinless, chopped	1	teaspoon onion flakes
1	cup mayonnaise	1	teaspoon cayenne
1	cup Parmesan cheese, grated	1	teaspoon parsley flakes
			paprika

Preheat oven 350°. Spray loaf pan or oven-proof casserole dish with nonstick spray.

Combine all ingredients in medium sized mixing bowl. Place mixture in baking dish. Bake at 350° for 20 to 25 minutes until bubbly and lightly browned on top.

Garnish with paprika, and serve with crackers.

Duck, turkey, pheasant or dove meat can be substituted.

Beer Battered Beaver With BBQ Dipping Sauce

Makes 50 servings

5	pounds beaver meat (no tails!) cut in pieces, cubed	2	12-ounce cans beer
1	gallon salted water	4	cups flour for dredging
4	tablespoons vinegar	4	cups vegetable oil for frying

Soak the cut up beaver overnight in the refrigerator in the salt water (1 cup salt to 1 gallon water), vinegar and beer.

Continued on Page 11

Beer Batter:

¾ cup flour
2 whole eggs, separated
1½ teaspoons salt
2 tablespoons vegetable oil

¾ cup beer, room temperature
freshly ground pepper,
to taste
flour for dredging

Place flour in bowl and add egg yolks, salt, oil, beer and a twist or two of freshly ground pepper. Stir with a whisk. Cover bowl with plastic wrap and allow to stand 2 to 24 hours refrigerated. Reserve egg whites in separate bowl until ready to fry the beaver. Whip egg whites until stiff, stir reserved batter, and fold beaten egg whites into the batter.

Cooking the Beaver: Remove beaver pieces from the marinade, dredge in flour, and dip into beer batter. Drop into a deep fryer or pot with oil heated to 360°. Fry beaver until golden brown and pieces float to the top. Remove beaver with a slotted spoon and drain on absorbent paper. Serve hot, with BBQ Dipping Sauce.

BBQ Dipping Sauce

Makes 2 cups

½ cup ketchup
¼ cup apple cider vinegar
½ cup vegetable oil
2 tablespoons light brown sugar
½ envelope dry onion soup mix
1 tablespoon stone-ground mustard

1 teaspoon prepared horseradish
¼ teaspoon garlic powder
½ cup water
1 tablespoon liquid Barbecue Smoke®
1 tablespoon Tabasco® sauce, or to taste

Combine all ingredients in a small saucepan; bring to a boil; lower heat and simmer about 10 minutes. Cool before using. May be made a day ahead. Reheat before serving.

Duck Bouchées with Soy Sauce

Makes 24 servings

1 ½ pounds duck, quail or dove, diced fine
8 tablespoons soy sauce
4 tablespoons Muscat wine or sweet white wine
1 teaspoon ground ginger

1 ½ teaspoons Chinese five-spice powder
salt and pepper to taste
6 tablespoons dry white wine
peanut oil for frying

Use a food processor with a metal blade. Combine the poultry, 2 tablespoons of soy sauce, 2 tablespoons of Muscat, the ginger, five-spice powder and salt and pepper to taste. Process at medium speed until it forms a fine texture.

Remove mixture and shape into individual walnut-sized balls. To ease the forming, continually dampen your hands with cold water.

In a small bowl, stir together the remaining Muscat, soy sauce and white wine. Reserve.

Heat 2 to 4 tablespoons of the oil in a large non-stick frying pan over medium heat. Arrange half of the meatballs in the pan and cook until golden brown, carefully turning to brown all sides, about 10 to 15 minutes. Remove meatballs to a plate and reserve. Add additional oil and cook the remaining meatballs the same way.

Remove the meatballs from the plate and discard any oil from the plate or frying pan. Pour the soy-wine mixture into the pan and return all meatballs to the pan.

Cook over high heat moving the pan in circular motions until almost all of the sauce evaporates and the meatballs are coated with an amber glaze.

Transfer to a serving platter and serve hot, warm or at room temperature.

Duck Quiches

Makes 18 servings

8	ounces pastry dough	¼	cup chopped green onions
3	large eggs	¾	cup heavy cream
½	teaspoon ground nutmeg	1	cup cooked duck meat, diced
	salt and pepper to taste		fine

This can be prepared with any finely chopped cooked wild game or fowl.

Remove the pastry dough from the refrigerator at least 30 minutes before you are ready to roll it out. Preheat oven to 425°.

On a lightly floured surface roll out the dough as thinly as possible. With fluted cutter, about 1¼-inch in diameter, cut out 18 rounds. Use these rounds to line 18 individual tartlet pans or a mini-muffin pan.

Break the eggs into a bowl. Add the nutmeg, salt and pepper to taste, green onions and beat with a fork until completely smooth. Continuing to beat, add the cream in a thin, steady stream. Distribute the diced duck evenly among the pastry lined pans, then pour in the cream mixture over each tart. Place the quiches in the oven and bake until filling sets and the crusts are golden, about 15 minutes.

These can be prepared ahead of time, then frozen and reheated at 350° for 10 minutes, or until hot.

Game Meat Balls

Makes 36 servings

1	pound antelope, elk or venison, ground	2	tablespoons Italian seasoning
¼	pound pork, ground	2	teaspoons prepared mustard
¼	cup breadcrumbs	1	tablespoon Worcestershire Sauce
¼	cup onion, finely chopped		
½	teaspoon salt	¼	cup cocktail sauce
½	teaspoon garlic powder	½	teaspoon Tabasco® sauce
		1	cup vegetable oil for frying

Combine all ingredients except oil in a mixing bowl, shape the mixture into small balls. Using a tablespoon for each. Heat vegetable oil in a skillet over medium heat, cook balls turning frequently. Brown on all sides, 5 to 8 minutes. Drain on paper towels. Serve with your favorite sweet and sour sauce, BBQ sauce or brown gravy.

Game Sausage Rolls

Makes 50 servings

1	sheet frozen puff pastry, preferably Pepperidge Farm	1	pound cooked game sausage, ground and seasoned
			ice water

Thaw pastry 20 minutes. On a lightly floured surface, roll to a 15½-inch x 9-inch rectangle. Cut rectangle into 3 long strips, each 3-inch wide.

Divide sausage meat into thirds; roll each into a snake the length of the pastry. Place each roll along one edge of a pastry strip. roll the pastry around the sausage. Wet edges with ice water and press to seal tightly. Chill the rolls for 1 hour. Preheat oven to 400°. Cut sausage rolls into ¾-inch slices and place on ungreased baking sheets. Bake for 10 to 12 minutes, or until pastry is puffed and golden. Serve warm or at room temperature.

Game Sausage Stuffed Mushrooms

Makes 36 servings

36 medium fresh mushrooms	¼ cup breadcrumbs
½ pound venison or other game sausage	2 tablespoons fresh chopped parsley
¾ cup Pepper Jack cheese, grated	1 large egg white

Preheat oven to 450°. Wash and remove stems from mushroom caps. Finely chop stems.

In a large non-stick skillet, combine stems and sausage. Cook over medium heat for 5 to 7 minutes or until meat is browned.

Remove from heat. Stir in cheese, breadcrumbs and parsley.

Arrange mushroom caps, stem side up in a greased casserole dish. Spoon about a tablespoon of game mixture into each cap.

Bake for 8 to 10 minutes until cheese is melted.

Marinated Frog Legs with "Creolaise" Sauce

Makes 24 servings

4 large eggs plus 2 tablespoons water	½ cup flour
2 cups Italian seasoned breadcrumbs	12 jumbo frog legs, split
	3 cups vegetable oil

Soak frog legs in marinade (page 16) at least 12 hours. Beat eggs in a medium bowl. Add water and beat again. Place Italian breadcrumbs on one plate and flour on another. Remove frog legs from marinade. Dust each one with flour, then dip in beaten egg, wash and roll in Italian breadcrumbs. Place on wire cake rack. Refrigerate for 30 minutes to set the breading. Heat vegetable oil to 360° in deep skillet and fry the frog legs until golden brown. Drain on paper towels and serve with Creolaise Dipping Sauce (page 16).

Frog Leg Marinade

Makes 1¼ cups

½ cup olive oil
1   tablespoon chopped parsley
½ cup white wine
1   tablespoon minced garlic
1   teaspoon creole/blackening
    seasoning

2   tablespoons green onions
1   tablespoon Worcestershire
    sauce
1   teaspoon chipotle sauce or
    Tabasco®

Combine marinade ingredients in large bowl. Add frog legs, turn to coat well, and cover. Marinate, refrigerated overnight, for at least 12 hours.

Creolaise Dipping Sauce

Makes 1 cup

2   egg yolks
1   tablespoon fresh lemon
    juice
¼ rounded teaspoon salt
⅛ teaspoon cayenne
2   teaspoons water

1   stick butter, melted and
    warm
1   tablespoon whole grain
    Creole mustard
2   teaspoons parsley, finely
    chopped

This is a basic hollandaise sauce, modified with Creole seasonings. In a double boiler or stainless steel bowl set over a pot of simmering water on medium heat, whisk the egg yolks with lemon juice, salt, cayenne and water until pale yellow and slightly thick. (Be careful not to let the bowl touch the water, as it might get too hot and set the eggs.) As soon as the eggs begin to thicken, remove the bowl from the pot and, whisking quickly, add the butter, 1 teaspoon at a time, until well blended. Add the Creole mustard and chopped parsley and serve immediately with the frog legs.

Marinated Aborigine Kangaroo Kabobs

Makes 25 servings

2	pounds kangaroo loin	25	bamboo skewers, soaked in
50	pearl onions, cooked		water

Cut kangaroo into strips 4-inch long. Marinate in Aborigine Marinade. While kangaroo marinates, simmer the onions in a little water, until softened, but not mushy; drain. Remove strips from marinade and weave in and out on bamboo skewers, putting a pearl onion on bottom and top of each skewer. Broil kabobs over charcoal fire or preheated gas grill until cooked through, turning only once. After turning, brush lightly with reserved boiled Aborigine marinade.

To Serve: Strain reserved marinade. Bring to a boil to remove any impurities and thicken with cornstarch or arrowroot. Brush kabobs with thickened marinade. Place extra sauce in bowl for dipping.

Aborigine Marinade and Sauce

Makes 3 quarts

4	cups chicken stock	2	tablespoons black pepper
1½	cups honey	2	teaspoons red pepper flakes,
1	cup mango puree		crushed
2½	cups ketchup	1	tablespoon fresh minced
5	cloves garlic, crushed		ginger
2	cups soy sauce	4	bay leaves
1	cup orange juice		

Mix all ingredients for marinade and heat to simmer. Remove from heat and allow to cool. Pour over kangaroo strips. Cover and refrigerate for 24 hours.

Mini Pizzas with Game Sausage

Makes 24

14   ounces pizza dough,
       prepared, not cooked
½   cup tomato sauce
1   cup mozzarella cheese,
       grated
1½ cups ground game sausage,
       already cooked

2   tablespoons extra virgin
       olive oil
1   teaspoon dried oregano
       freshly ground pepper to
       taste
1   pound plum tomatoes,
       seeded and cut thin
       grated Parmesan cheese

Have the pizza dough ready. Preheat oven to 500°.

On a lightly floured surface, roll out the dough ¼-inch thick. With a pastry cutter 1½-inch diameter, cut out 24 rounds. Now roll these rounds out individually to ³⁄₁₆-inch thick. Lay the rounds on a non-stick baking sheet.

Form a small rim around each round, to contain the filling.

Place the tomato sauce in a bowl. Add the mozzarella and game sausage. Drizzle with the olive oil, sprinkle with the oregano and pepper to taste.

Mix gently. Divide the tomato mixture evenly among the dough rounds and top each with a plum tomato round and a little Parmesan cheese. Place baking sheet in oven and bake until the cheese melts and the edges of the crust are golden brown, about 10 to 15 minutes. Watch carefully to prevent burning.

Quail Canapes

Makes 30 servings

Crust:

8 ounces cream cheese, softened

1 cup butter, softened

2 cups all-purpose flour

Filling:

3½ cups quail meat, skinless, cooked and cubed

⅓ cup White Cheddar cheese, shredded

⅓ cup celery, thinly sliced

⅓ cup mayonnaise

3 tablespoons green onion, chopped

2 tablespoons sour cream

¼ teaspoon cinnamon

¼ teaspoon salt

¼ teaspoon pepper

Heat oven to 400°. In medium mixing bowl, cut cream cheese and butter into flour until soft dough forms. Cover with plastic and refrigerate for 1 hour.

Shape dough into 30 balls, about 2-inch in diameter. Press each ball into bottom and up sides of mini muffin cups. Bake for 8 to 10 minutes, or until golden brown.

In large mixing bowl, combine all filling ingredients. Spoon about 1 tablespoon of quail mixture into each pastry shell. Bake for 5 minutes or until cheese is melted.

You may substitute any wild game bird meat for the quail, including turkey, pheasant or dove. These freeze well and can be made ahead of time.

Tex-Mex Game Wontons

Makes 48 servings

½	pound ground game meat	1	tablespoon catsup
¼	cup onion, chopped	1½	teaspoons chili powder
2	tablespoons green pepper, chopped	¼	teaspoon ground cumin
½	15-ounce can refried beans	4	dozen wonton wrappers
½	cup cheddar cheese, shredded		frying oil
			Salsa of your choice

For filling, in a large skillet cook ground game meat, onion, and green pepper until meat is brown and vegetables are tender. Drain off fat. Stir beans, cheese, catsup, chili powder, and cumin into meat mixture. Mix well. Place a wonton wrapper on work surface with one point toward you. Spoon a generous tablespoon of meat mixture onto center of wrapper. Fold bottom point of wonton wrapper over filling; tuck point under filling. Fold side corners over, forming an envelope shape. Roll up toward remaining corner, moisten point with drop of water and seal. Repeat with remaining wonton wrappers and filling. Fry a few at a time in a deep fryer, heated to 375°, about 1 minute per side. Use a slotted spoon to remove wontons. Drain on paper towels. Serve with your choice of salsa.

These can be made ahead of time and reheated in a 350° oven for 10 to 12 minutes.

Wild Boar Satay With Indonesian Peanut Sauce

Makes 30 Satays

3	pounds wild boar, trimmed lean	30	bamboo skewers

Cut wild boar into 1-inch cubes. Blend all ingredients for Bulgogi marinade. Place boar cubes in marinade for 8 to 24 hours, refrigerated. Soak skewers in water for at least 20 minutes before threading. After marinating, place 3 cubes of boar on each 6-inch skewer and lay in sheet pan to allow to drain. Reserve some of the marinade, after the meat is taken out, and bring it to a boil to remove any impurities.

Cooking the Satays:
Prepare a hot charcoal fire or preheat gas grill. Brush grilling surface with oil, then place satays on grill to cook. When one side is brown, turn and cook the other side, approximately 4 to 6 minutes each side. Do not turn more than once. After turning, brush lightly with reserved boiled Bulgogi Marinade. Serve with Indonesian Peanut Dipping Sauce.

Indonesian Peanut Dipping Sauce

Makes 1 ¼ cups

1	clove garlic, minced	1	teaspoon salt
1	tablespoon peanut oil	2	tablespoons sugar
1	teaspoon dried red chile peppers, soaked	1	cup smooth peanut butter
2	teaspoons tamarind paste, dissolved in 2 tablespoons water		

This dipping sauce can be made one day ahead. Sauté the garlic in peanut oil until light brown. Add soaked chile peppers, tamarind liquid, salt and sugar. When mixture starts to simmer, add peanut butter until blended. Store at room temperature. Serve with Wild Boar Satay.

Bulgogi Marinade

Makes 2 cups

1 cup soy sauce
½ cup water
3 tablespoons green onion, chopped
3 teaspoons garlic, minced
1 tablespoon sugar

3 teaspoons fresh ginger, minced
1 tablespoon black pepper
2 tablespoons sesame seeds, toasted and ground
2 tablespoons olive oil

Blend all ingredients for marinade. Place meat cubes in marinade for 8 to 24 hours, refrigerated.

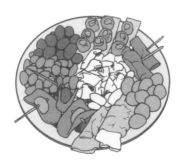

Wild Duck Pâté

Makes 1 loaf pan or 40 hors d'oeuvres

½	pound duck meat pieces	¼	teaspoon allspice
¼	medium onion, rough chopped	¼	teaspoon ground ginger
¼	cup duck/chicken fat	3	tablespoons brandy (jigger)
3	whole eggs	2	tablespoons flour
1¼	teaspoons salt	¼	cup heavy cream
½	teaspoon white pepper		aspic

This is a pâté that can be made in an electric blender or food processor!

Cut duck meat into small pieces, making sure to remove all skin, bone and shot. Place in blender with onion, fat, eggs and spices. Blend at high speed for about 5 minutes. Add brandy, flour and cream and mix on low speed until mixture is well blended. about 1 minute. Select mold to be used; pâté may be poured into small individual muffin tins, large muffin tins, rectangular loaf pan, stainless steel bowl or into various metal pudding molds. Grease molds with butter or shortening. Pour liquid mixture from blender/food processor into mold. Cover filled mold(s) with foil and place in a water bath in oven. Poach at 300° in oven. Small individual molds will take about 20 minutes; a large mold will take about half an hour. The cooked pâté will have a light, spongy consistency. Unmold pâté while it is warm, but not hot.

Aspic:

Chill well. Wash and dry pâté mold. Replace pâté in mold. Dissolve one tablespoon (1 packet) plain gelatin in two tablespoons brandy. Add one cup boiling chicken stock and one tablespoon lemon juice. Stir until dissolved. Pour gelatin mixture through a fine strainer or cheesecloth to remove impurities. Pour mixture around pâté in mold. Wrap in foil; chill until firm. To serve, unmold pâté by running back of mold under hot water to loosen aspic; turn out onto platter or individual plates. Decorate as desired. Makes 1 cup gelatin-aspic mixture; may be increased in direct proportions.

Wild Duck Spring Rolls

Makes 14 Rolls

2	pounds wild duck, dressed	½	teaspoon ginger, grated
8	cups water	1	tablespoon Chinese Five
1	cup celery, sliced		Spice powder
2	bay leaves	1	tablespoon cornstarch
6	peppercorns	2	tablespoons dry sherry
2	cups cabbage, shredded	2	tablespoons soy sauce
½	cup water chestnuts, drained and chopped	1	tablespoon sesame oil
2	tablespoons green onion, chopped	14	egg roll wrappers, 7-inch square
½	cup carrot, shredded	1	egg yolk
		2 to 4	cups vegetable oil

In a 6- to 8-quart Dutch oven or stockpot, combine duck pieces, water, celery, bay leaves, and peppercorns. Bring to a boil over medium high heat. Reduce heat to medium. Cook for 30 to 45 minutes, or until meat is tender and falling off the bones. Remove duck from the broth. Cool slightly. Chop or shred meat. Discard bones and skin. Strain broth and keep for a future use.

In a large mixing bowl, combine shredded meat, cabbage, water chestnuts, green onions, carrots, ginger root, five spice powder, cornstarch, sherry, soy sauce and sesame oil.

Place 2 heaping tablespoons of wild duck mixture, just below center of each egg roll wrapper. Roll up, folding in sides, Brush with egg yolk and 1 tablespoon of water mixed together; continue rolling to completely seal.

In a wok or deep non-stick skillet, heat oil over medium high heat. Cook spring rolls 4 at a time, for 3 to 4 minutes, or until golden brown, turning once.

Drain on paper towel lined plate or platter. Serve spring rolls with sweet and sour sauce, hot mustard, soy sauce or plum sauce.

Antlered Game

Antlered Game Pot Roast

Makes 8 servings

1	large venison, antelope, elk rump roast or shoulder	1	tablespoon garlic, minced
	flour seasoned with ground pepper	2	cups canned tomatoes
		2	bay leaves
	bacon drippings or oil	½	teaspoon dried thyme
2	large carrots, sliced	½	teaspoon ground cloves
2	stalks celery, chopped	¼	teaspoon ground allspice
2	large onions, sliced		parsley sprigs for garnish

Coat the meat on all sides with seasoned flour. Heat bacon drippings in Dutch oven over high heat. Brown roast, turning to sear all sides. If bacon drippings are not available, use vegetable oil.

Add carrots, celery, onions and garlic during the last few minutes of the browning process. Add tomatoes, herbs and spices. Cover and simmer very slowly. The liquid needs to barely bubble. Check occasionally to make sure there is enough liquid; if not, add beef stock or additional water. Cook at least 4 to 5 hours, until tender. Remove meat to a hot platter, discard bay leaves and reserve all remaining ingredients. Put sauce and cooked vegetables in a food processor or blender and puree to thicken.

To finish: Return puree to pot and reheat to boiling. Serve pot roast sliced with sauce on the side. Boiled potatoes and additional carrots are a nice accompaniment. Garnish with parsley.

Game Picadillo

Makes 6 servings

1	medium onion, chopped	½	teaspoon ground allspice
1	clove garlic, minced	2	cups canned tomatoes
2	tablespoons oil	2	tablespoons red wine vinegar
2	pounds ground game meat (elk, venison or antelope)	2	tablespoons raisins
		¾	teaspoon salt
3	teaspoons red pepper flakes	¾	teaspoon pepper
1	tablespoon dried oregano	½	cup fresh cilantro, chopped,
1	tablespoon ground cumin		for garnish
½	teaspoon ground coriander		

In a large skillet, sauté onion and garlic in the oil until onion is golden, but not brown. Add ground game meat, red pepper flakes, oregano, cumin, coriander and allspice.

Cook, stirring occasionally, until meat is thoroughly browned. Mix in tomatoes, vinegar, raisins, salt and pepper. Cook over low heat until liquid is reduced by half. Garnish with chopped fresh cilantro. This is traditionally served with rice and black beans.

Venison Sausage

Makes 5 logs

5	pounds deer burger	4	teaspoons mustard seed
5	teaspoons Morton Tender Quick Salt	5	teaspoons coarse black pepper
		2	teaspoon cayenne pepper
3	teaspoons garlic salt	1	teaspoon liquid smoke
6	teaspoons hickory smoke salt	1	tablespoon Accent/MSG

Wash hands. Mix everything together well, using hands. Put mixture in a big covered bowl in refrigerator. For 5 days, "work" sausage with clean hands – once each day. On the 5th day, shape into logs, about 1 1/2 to 2 inches in diameter. Bake logs on a broiler pan for 8 hours at 150°F. Turn only once after first 4 hours of baking. Wrap and chill. Serve sliced with mustard on the side. Keeps well for 2-3 weeks. May also be frozen.

Antelope in Puff Pastry Shells

Makes 8 servings

2½ to 3 pounds antelope round, cubed
5 to 6 slices bacon, diced
  flour for dredging
1⅓ cups onion, chopped
4 cloves garlic, chopped
1⅓ cups dry red wine
1⅓ cups water
2½ tablespoons demi-glace or dark brown gravy
⅛ teaspoon allspice
2 bay leaves
⅓ teaspoon thyme
  freshly ground black pepper

  paprika
3 cups cabbage, chopped
24 pearl onions
1½ cups green peas
1½ cups mushroom, sliced
⅔ cup heavy cream
2½ teaspoons cornstarch, optional, dissolved in a little water
8 individual puff pastry shells, already baked

In a large pot, fry the diced bacon and remove with a slotted spoon. Dredge antelope in flour and brown in bacon fat on all sides. Add the onion and garlic and lightly sauté. Add the red wine, water, demi-glace, allspice, bay leaves, thyme and a sprinkling of black pepper and paprika. Return the bacon to the pot and add the cabbage; simmer for 2 to 3 hours, stirring occasionally, until meat is tender. Add the pearl onions, peas and mushrooms and cook for another 15 minutes. Then add the heavy cream and simmer another 10 minutes; thicken with cornstarch, if the sauce is too thin. Ladle into individual heated puff pastry shells and serve.

Note: Puff pastry shells are available in the freezer section of better supermarkets. Bake according to package directions.

Backwoods Antelope Ragout

Makes 8 servings

½	pound sliced bacon	½	cup beer	
3	pounds antelope, cut into small cubes	2	tablespoons bourbon	
		1	teaspoon curry powder	
3	medium onions, chopped		salt and pepper	
5	cloves garlic, chopped	1	cup fresh mushrooms, sliced	
1½	quarts water		salt and pepper to taste	
1	10-ounce can tomato soup			

Cook the bacon in a Dutch oven, crumble and set aside. Pour off all but ¼ cup bacon fat. Brown meat in the bacon fat and set aside. Brown the onions and garlic in the same pot, then add the water, tomato soup, beer, bourbon, curry powder salt and pepper. Bring to boil and put the meat and bacon back into pot. Reduce to very low, cover and simmer for 1 to 2 hours, or until meat is very tender. When meat is tender, add mushrooms and simmer an additional 15 minutes. Excellent served over egg noodles.

Antelope/Elk Creole Style

Makes 8 servings

4 pounds antelope or elk stew meat, marinated
5 tablespoons butter

Cut antelope or elk into 16 4-ounce medallions/pieces. Marinate for 12 to 24 hours in Antelope/Elk Creole Style Marinade (page 30).

Heat 5 tablespoons of butter in heavy skillet, until melted. Remove antelope/elk from marinade and brown on both sides. Remove and reserve. Make Creole Sauce (page 30). Add meat to the sauce and simmer 30 minutes or until tender. Serve two medallions per plate over rice or mashed potatoes.

Antelope/Elk Creole Style Marinade

Makes 1¼ cups

½ cup Southern Comfort
    Whiskey
1 tablespoon
    Creole/blackening seasoning
½ cup olive oil
1 teaspoon basil

1 teaspoon rosemary
1 teaspoon marjoram
1 tablespoon garlic, minced
    salt and pepper

Combine all marinade ingredients and marinate meat in refrigerator for 12 to 24 hours.

Antelope/Elk Creole Sauce

Makes 1½ quarts

1 tablespoon vegetable oil
½ cup onion, chopped
½ cup celery, chopped
2 cups mixed bell peppers
    (green, yellow, red), chopped
1 tablespoon garlic, minced
1 cup diced stewed tomatoes

1 tablespoons Creole /
    blackening seasoning
2 tablespoons Italian
    seasoning
2 cups chicken stock
1 cup white wine

In heavy skillet, combine vegetable oil, onion, celery, peppers and garlic sauté until soft. Add tomatoes, Creole seasoning and Italian seasoning. Stir to blend. Add chicken stock and white wine and bring to a simmer. Add antelope/elk to the sauce and simmer 30 minutes or until tender.

Antelope & Elk Burritos with Sauce Mexicana

Makes 8 servings

1   pound antelope, in large cubes
1   large onion, sliced
2   cloves garlic, chopped
2   tablespoons red wine vinegar
2   cups beef stock
1   16-ounce can tomatoes, crushed
1   pound elk, in large cubes

3   whole red and/or green bell peppers, julienned
2   cups whole kernel corn (frozen or fresh)
2   tablespoons olive oil
8   10-inch flour tortillas, warmed
4   green onions, chopped, for garnish
    Sauce Mexicana

In a large pot or Dutch oven, bring the meat to a boil with the onion, garlic, vinegar and beef stock. Cover and simmer over a low heat for 2 or 3 hours. After the first hour, add the crushed tomatoes. They should simmer with the meat for at least 45 minutes. When the meat is very, very, tender, remove it with a slotted spoon and shred it on a plate. when all the meat is shredded, return it to the stock. Meanwhile, sauté the bell peppers and corn in the olive oil until very tender. Add vegetables to meat, and heat uncovered until almost all liquid is evaporated.

Place about ¾ cup of the meat filling in the middle of a tortilla; turn up on end to form a flap, which stops the filling from falling out; and roll up. Repeat until all the tortillas are filled. Garnish each serving with Sauce Mexicana (page 32), and a few chopped green onions.

Sauce Mexicana

Makes 8 servings

¾ cup vegetable oil
4 dried chipotle peppers
1 dried ancho chile
2 white onions, peeled and quartered
⅓ cup olive oil
2 thick onion slices
salt and pepper to taste

4 medium garlic cloves, peeled
salt
25 tomatillos, fresh or canned
½ cup fresh cilantro, chopped

Heat vegetable oil over medium heat in large skillet. Sauté chipotles and ancho briefly to soften—approximately 3 minutes. Remove chiles/peppers and drain. In same pan, add garlic and onions and brown, adding a pinch or two of salt. Remove onions and garlic to a bowl. If using fresh tomatillos, remove the papery husks. In blender or food processor, puree tomatillos. Add chiles, onions, peppers and garlic and puree again. Add cilantro and pulse several times. Reserve sauce.

In large saucepan, heat olive oil and brown the two thick onion slices until browned to season the pan. Remove onions and discard (or save for another use). Add sauce to the pan and cook over low heat for 30 to 45 minutes to blend all flavors. Correct seasoning, adding salt and pepper to taste. Serve with Antelope & Elk Burritos (page 31).

Elk Curry

Makes 4 servings

1 pound elk meat, cubed
3 tablespoons peanut oil
1 tablespoon turmeric

1 tablespoon ground cumin
1 tablespoon freshly ground pepper

(Continued on Page 33)

Elk Curry *(Continued from previous page)*:

1	tablespoon fresh ginger, minced	1	large onion, chopped
½	tablespoon salt	2	cloves garlic, minced
		½	cup game stock or beef stock

Cut the meat into bite size cubes or strips, reserve. Heat peanut oil in heavy skillet. In small bowl combine the turmeric and all other spices ... mix well. Dredge meat in spice mixture.

Add meat, frying until it becomes brown. Add the onion and garlic and cook 5 minutes. Then add the stock. Simmer gently for approximately 30 minutes or until the meat is tender and the sauce has thickened slightly. Serve over rice or noodles.

Elk Loaf With Sun-Dried Tomato & Corn Salsa

Makes 8 servings

1 ½	cups finely crushed corn tortilla chips	2	eggs
1	cup milk	5	tablespoons fresh parsley, chopped
1 ½	pounds ground elk	2	tablespoons fresh parsley, chopped, for garnish
3	cups sun-dried tomato and corn salsa (page 34)		

Soak the corn chips in milk until soft; combine with the elk, add 1 cup of the Sun-Dried tomato and Corn Salsa, without the corn. Add the eggs; combine well. Pack into a loaf pan or shape into a loaf in a shallow baking dish. Combine remaining salsa with cilantro, parsley and corn. Spoon over the loaf. Bake in a 350° oven for 1 hour. Serve with additional salsa, if desired. Garnish with parsley. Venison or antelope can be substituted for the elk and is also very good.

Sun-Dried Tomato and Corn Salsa

Makes 3 cups

1	cup sun-dried tomatoes	4	tablespoons cilantro, minced
	water to cover	2	tablespoons lemon or lime
¼	cup onion, finely chopped		juice
2	cloves garlic, minced		salt and pepper to taste
2	cups boiling water	½	cup whole kernel corn,
2	large ripe tomatoes, chopped		cooked or roasted
3	serrano peppers, seeded and		
	minced		

Soak sun-dried tomatoes in water until soft and chop. Put chopped onion and garlic into a colander and pour 2 cups of boiling water over them; drain thoroughly; discard water. Let cool. Combine sun-dried tomatoes, fresh tomatoes, peppers, cilantro and lemon juice with the onions and garlic, adding salt and pepper to taste. Refrigerate to allow flavors to blend. Add roasted corn kernels after using part of this salsa in the elk loaf.

Grilled Marinated Venison Steaks

Makes 8 servings

4	pounds boneless loin of	¾	cup Venison Steak Marinade
	venison		salt and pepper to taste

Cut venison into steaks about 1-inch thick. Place in glass or enameled pan large enough to hold steaks as well as marinade. Cover steaks with marinade (page 35) and let marinate for 24 hours. Remove steaks from the marinade and grill over hot charcoal or on a hot, preheated gas grill. Steaks should be cooked rare to medium. (Note: Well-done venison steak may be tough.)

Meanwhile, pour leftover marinade into a pot and reduce by half.

Skim top of liquid to remove any impurities. Keep marinade warm to use as a sauce with the venison steaks.

Venison Steak Marinade

Makes 8 servings

¼ cup juniper berries, crushed
4 sprigs fresh rosemary
2 tablespoons black
   peppercorns, crushed
1 cup red wine

3   cloves garlic, crushed
3   shallots, chopped
1½   cups Italian-style vinaigrette
½   cup A-1® Steak Sauce
½   cup soy sauce

Combine the marinade ingredients and pour over the venison steaks in flat dish to cover completely. Wrap tightly with plastic or foil and place in refrigerator for at least 24 hours.

Grilled Venison Steaks with Jalapeño Sauce

Makes 4 servings

4 venison steaks, ½-inch to
   ¾-inch thick, loin cut,
   trimmed

Marinate venison steaks in Jalapeño Marinade (page 36), 6 to 12 hours. Remove marinated venison from refrigerator. Preheat gas grill or prepare charcoal for grilling. Grill venison as you would your favorite steak. Serve steaks brushed lightly with heated Jalapeño Sauce (page 36). If desired, serve additional heated sauce on the side. Grill to medium/medium rare for best results, as well-done steaks may be tough.

Jalapeño Marinade

Makes 1 cup

1	tablespoon olive oil
¼	cup red wine
1	tablespoon Worcestershire sauce
1	teaspoon fresh thyme, chopped
1	tablespoon kosher salt
3	tablespoons cracked pepper
3	tablespoons garlic, minced
3	tablespoons jalapeño peppers, minced

Whisk together the marinade ingredients and cover both sides of steaks with the mixture. Cover and allow to marinate in the refrigerator for 6 to 12 hours.

Jalapeño Sauce

Makes 3 cups

22	jalapeños, stemmed, cut crosswise, seeded (about 2 cups)
3	cloves garlic, sliced
½	cup thinly sliced onion
¾	teaspoon salt
1	tablespoon sugar
1	teaspoon vegetable oil
2	cups water
1	cup apple cider vinegar

Combine the jalapeños, garlic, onions, salt, sugar and oil in saucepan over high heat. Sauté for 3 to 5 minutes. Add water and continue to cook stirring often, for about 2 minutes. Remove from the heat and allow to steep until mixture cools completely. Once cooled, puree the mixture in batches in a blender for 15 to 20 seconds, or until very smooth. With the blender running, pour the vinegar through the feed tube in a steady stream. Pour sauce into a sterilized jar and secure with airtight lid. Refrigerate. Best if aged 2 to 3 weeks before using. May be stored up to 4 months in the refrigerator.

Venison Steak with Bing Cherry Relish

Makes 8 servings

8   loin venison steaks cut 1-inch thick, marinated in Jalapeño Marinade (page 36)

Grill venison steaks over a hot charcoal fire or preheated gas grill to desired doneness. Serve topped with Bing Cherry Relish (about ¼ cup per serving).

Bing Cherry Relish

Makes 8 servings

1½ cups bing cherries, pitted	1 tablespoon cilantro, finely chopped
½ medium red onion, diced	
½ medium green onion, sliced	1 teaspoon orange zest, finely chopped
½ medium green bell pepper, seeded and chopped	⅓ cup orange juice
½ medium jalapeño pepper, seeded and minced (leave seeds in if you like it hot!	1 tablespoon Dijon mustard
	1½ teaspoons ground cumin
	¼ cup canola oil
3 tablespoons raisins, plumped	salt to taste

In large bowl, combine cherries, red onion, green onion, bell pepper, jalapeño pepper, raisins, cilantro and orange zest. In a food processor or blender, combine orange juice, mustard and cumin until smooth. With the machine running, gradually add the oil in a very thin stream; mixture will thicken. Pour dressing over the cherry mixture. Toss gently. Season to taste with salt. Cover and refrigerate at least 2 to 4 hours before serving.

Venison Steaks with Jalapeño Orange Butter

Makes 4 servings

1	tablespoon olive oil	4	8-ounce loin venison steaks,
¼	cup red wine		½-inch to ¾-inch thick,
1	tablespoon Worcestershire		trimmed
	sauce	1	tablespoon kosher salt
1	teaspoon fresh thyme,	½	tablespoon cracked black
	chopped		pepper

Whisk together the oil, wine, Worcestershire and thyme, cover both sides of the steaks with the mixture and allow to marinate for 6 to 12 hours. Heat a cast iron skillet until a drop of water sizzles on the surface. Drain venison, season with salt and pepper and add to the hot pan in a single layer. Brown well, turn over and brown the other side. Remove the steaks from the pan and keep warm. Add the left over marinade to the pan and allow to reduce a little. Pour a little reduced marinade over the warm steaks. Top each steak with a tablespoon of jalapeño orange butter and serve while the butter is melting.

Overcooking venison steaks may result in tough meat ... best served at medium to medium rare.

Jalapeño Orange Butter

Makes ⅔ cup

¼	cup unsalted butter, room temperature	2	tablespoons canned jalapeño, minced
⅛	cup orange marmalade with zest, room temperature	2	tablespoons fresh cilantro, coarsely chopped

Stir together the butter and the marmalade. Add the jalapeño and cilantro. Portion into tablespoon-size servings and refrigerate, tightly wrapped. This can be made 2 days ahead. Any left over portions can be well-wrapped and frozen for future use. Bring to room temperature before serving.

Roasted Venison With Shallot Sauce

Makes 8 servings

1	6-pound venison roast	2	bay leaves, crushed
6	bacon slices	1	teaspoon thyme
1½	cups Cabernet Sauvignon or Red Burgundy wine	4	whole cloves
½	teaspoon black pepper	8	shallots, chopped
2	white onions, sliced	2	tablespoons butter
1	cup celery, diced		salt and pepper to taste
1	cup carrots, diced		
1	cup cilantro, chopped		

Lard or wrap the roast in bacon strips, securing with string. Combine all ingredients except shallots and butter to make marinade. Place roast in a covered pot and pour marinade over roast. Marinate covered in refrigerator for 48 hours, turning often. Preheat oven to 450°. Roast for 30 minutes, then turn oven down to 350° and continue to roast, basting often, until tender, 4 to 5 hours. Remove the meat from the pan and keep warm. Add shallots and butter to the pan. Bring to a boil and cook until shallots soften. For a thicker sauce, add a tablespoon of cornstarch that has been mixed with ¼ cup water and simmer for 5 minutes, then add a dash more of red wine. Let roast stand for 5 to 10 minutes for easier slicing. Serve sauce on the side.

Venetian Venison

Makes 6 servings

¼	cup olive oil	1	teaspoon dried oregano
5	whole garlic cloves, peeled	1	28-ounce can plum tomatoes
1½	pounds venison, cut in 1-inch cubes	1	28-ounce can tomato puree
1	medium onion, chopped		fresh parsley
1	6-ounce can tomato paste		freshly ground black pepper
5	basil leaves, torn or 2 teaspoons dried basil		romano cheese, freshly grated
1	teaspoon dried rosemary		pasta of your choice

In a heavy 8-quart dutch oven or pot with cover, heat the oil and slowly brown the garlic on all sides. Remove garlic and reserve. Add the venison cubes and brown on all sides; remove and reserve.

Add the onion and sauté until golden; add the tomato paste, basil, rosemary and oregano, and cook, stirring, about 5 minutes over low heat. Add the tomatoes, the tomato puree and one 28-ounce can filled with water; stir to blend. Return the garlic and the venison to the sauce, raise heat until the mixture reaches a boil, then lower it and simmer, partially covered, about 2 to 3 hours. Stir occasionally.

You should have a fairly thick sauce which will not be spicy, but rather sweet. Thin it with additional water as it cooks, if you prefer a thinner sauce.

Serve over your favorite pasta, topped with black pepper, parsley and grated romano cheese.

Venison à la Valerie with Forest Mushrooms

Makes 8 servings

1   4-pound venison roast
½   cup butter, plus additional for sautéing
1   cup red and green bell peppers, diced
2   cups onions, thinly sliced

2   cups forest mushrooms, thinly sliced (portobello, porcini, shittake, chanterelle, or button)
½   cup Cognac

Preheat oven to 450°.

For medium rare venison, roast 15 minutes per pound. Place roast in a heavy roasting pan and brush with ½ cup melted butter. Season with black pepper and roast 15 minutes. Reduce heat to 350° and continue to roast and baste, turning the meat occasionally.

When the roast is almost done, melt additional butter in a skillet and lightly sauté the peppers, onions and mushrooms together.

When roast is done, remove it to a heated platter to rest for 10 to 15 minutes. Pour the Cognac into the bottom of the roaster, and place on stove. Heat the pan over high heat, boiling and scraping up any of the baked-on drippings until Cognac is reduced by half. Stir well to blend. Add to the mixture of sautéed peppers, onions, and mushrooms; blend well, and serve warm over sliced roast venison.

Dried wild mushrooms can also be substituted for fresh.

Venison Lasagna

Makes 6 servings

1	pound venison, ground	3	tablespoons Italian seasoning
½	pound Italian pork sausage, ground	9 to 12	uncooked lasagna noodles
2	teaspoons onion salt	2	8-ounce containers ricotta cheese
2	teaspoons garlic salt		
1	16-ounce can crushed tomatoes	1½	teaspoons dried oregano leaves
1	15-ounce can tomato sauce	½	cup Parmesan cheese, grated
1	tablespoon sugar	2	cups mozzarella cheese, shredded

Preheat oven 350°.

Cook venison, sausage, onion and garlic salt in heavy skillet over medium heat until lightly browned. Drain. Add tomatoes with liquid, tomato sauce, sugar and Italian seasoning. Bring to boil, stirring occasionally. Reduce heat and simmer, uncovered, until mixture is thick, about 45 minutes.

Cook lasagna noodles as directed on package. Keep in bowl of cool water. Mix ricotta cheese, oregano and ¼ cup Parmesan cheese. Reserve.

Remove ½ cup of the sauce mixture and set aside for later. In an oblong baking pan, approximately 10-inches by 16-inches, you will be making three layers of noodles, sauce and cheese.

Place a thin layer of sauce on bottom of pan. Place 3 to 4 noodles on top of sauce, spread ⅓ of ricotta cheese mixture and sprinkle with ⅓ of the mozzarella. Repeat two more times with same ingredients. Put any additional cheese and sauce on top layer. Sprinkle with Parmesan cheese. Bake uncovered for 45 minutes. Let stand 15 minutes before cutting.

Venison Pasta Sauce

Makes 1 ½ quarts

½ pound Italian pork sausage
2 pounds venison, ground
1 ¼ cups beef/game stock
¼ cup Italian seasoning
2 cups water
2 tablespoons olive oil
2 medium onions, diced
1 green bell pepper, diced
1 red bell pepper, diced

2 cloves garlic, minced
½ cup red wine
2 ½ cups canned chopped
tomatoes
2 teaspoons black pepper
salt to taste
1 cup fresh mushrooms,
sliced

In a large frying pan brown the Italian sausage, breaking it up as it browns; remove and reserve. Add the ground venison to the same pan and sauté until brown. Return sausage to the pan along with the beef or game stock, Italian seasoning and water. Bring to a boil, lower the heat and simmer for 2 to 3 hours. Add a little water from time to time if needed. About 1 ½ hours before you want the sauce to be finished, heat the olive oil in a skillet. Sauté the onions, bell peppers, and garlic until softened and add to the meat mixture along with the red wine and tomatoes, stirring them into the sauce. Add salt and pepper, blending thoroughly. Raise the heat until the sauce bubbles. Lower the heat to simmer and continue to cook, stirring occasionally, for 1 hour. Then add the mushrooms and simmer 10 minutes. Serve over spaghetti or other pasta. Any leftover sauce may be frozen for future use.

Venison Stir-Fry

Makes 4 servings

4	tablespoons peanut oil	1	teaspoon red pepper flakes, optional
2	medium green peppers, julienned	½	cup water chestnuts, sliced
1	medium red pepper, julienned	1	pound boneless venison stew meat, cut across the grain and marinated at least 1 hour
1	medium yellow pepper, julienned		
1	cup snow peas		soy sauce to taste

Place all vegetables and venison in bowl and toss with Venison Stir-Fry Marinade (page 45). Marinate for at least 1 hour. Heat a wok or large cast iron skillet over high heat until very hot. Add 2 tablespoons peanut oil to the wok and immediately stir-fry the peppers, snow peas and water chestnuts, adding optional red pepper flakes. Cook until peppers and snow peas are tender, but still have a little texture. Remove vegetables and place in a bowl. Reserve. Add the rest of the peanut oil to the wok and repeat the process with the meat slices, turning them until they are browned. Add 3 tablespoons of the Venison Stir-Fry Marinade (page 45), bring to a simmer and return vegetables to pan. Mix meat and vegetables well and cook 1 minute. Add soy sauce to taste, if desired.

Serve over rice or noodles.

Venison Stir-Fry Marinade

Makes ½ cup

3	tablespoons soy sauce	2	tablespoons cornstarch
2	tablespoons sake or dry white wine	1	teaspoon sugar
1	teaspoon fresh ginger, minced	1	teaspoon black pepper
		1	tablespoon crushed black pepper

Mix the marinade ingredients in a casserole dish. Add the vegetables and meat slices, stir to coat the meat well. Let marinate at least 1 hour, turning frequently.

If marinating for more than 1 hour, refrigerate.

Venison Stuffed Peppers

Makes 6 servings

6	red, green or yellow bell peppers	1	teaspoon dried basil
1½	pounds ground venison or other game	1	teaspoon dried sage
			salt and pepper to taste
2	medium onions, chopped	2	cups marinara sauce
4	tablespoons bacon drippings	¼	cup water
1	cup cooked basmati rice	⅓	cup mozzarella cheese, shredded
2	teaspoons garlic, minced		

Preheat oven to 325°. Cut off stem end of bell peppers, remove seeds and white membrane; blanch in salted water 5 minutes, rinse in cold water and drain.

Brown ground venison and onion in bacon drippings. Combine with cooked rice, garlic, herbs and seasonings, Stuff blanched peppers with meat mixture, place in greased casserole dish. Mix marinara with water to thin. Pour thinned marinara sauce over and around the peppers. Top peppers with shredded mozzarella cheese. Bake 20 to 25 minutes uncovered.

Venison Vegetable Stew

Makes 6 servings

2	pounds venison, cubed	½	teaspoon dried thyme, crumbled
1	cup apple juice		
1	bay leaf	1	small piece cheese cloth and string
1	clove garlic, minced		
1	teaspoon salt	2	carrots, diced
1	tablespoon black pepper	1	cup green peas
2	tablespoons bacon drippings or oil	1	cup potato, peeled and diced cornstarch
2	celery stalks, diced	2	tablespoons Jack Daniel's Tennessee Whiskey
8	whole cloves		
1	tablespoon parsley, chopped	1½	cups beef stock or game stock parsley sprigs for garnish

Place meat in deep bowl. Add apple juice, bay leaf, garlic, salt and pepper. Marinate, covered, in refrigerator for at least 4 hours, turning frequently.

Drain the meat, reserving the marinade. In a dutch oven, brown the meat thoroughly in the bacon drippings or oil over medium heat. Remove meat and reserve. Place 1 diced celery stalk, cloves, parsley and thyme in cheese cloth and tie with string. Add to the pot with beef stock and simmer 10 to 15 minutes.

Replace meat in pot, cover and simmer until tender, about 3 hours. Add remaining celery, carrots and potatoes during the final hour of cooking. Add peas during last five minutes of cooking. Add additional hot water if pot gets dry. Discard cheese cloth bag, remove meat and vegetables, and reserve. Use ½ tablespoon of cornstarch for each cup of broth. Add a little cold water to the cornstarch and make into a smooth paste before putting in stock. Add Jack Daniel's, boil broth, while stirring in cornstarch mixture to thicken the gravy. Place meat and vegetables in gravy and heat. Garnish with parsley sprigs, serve over rice or noodles.

Venison Sauerbraten

Makes 6 servings

1   venison roast about 2 to 2½ pounds
2   tablespons vegetable oil
6 to 8 ginger snaps, crushed

Marinade:

1	sliced onion	1	teaspoon juniper berries
2	bay leaves	2	cups red balsamic vinegar
12	peppercorns	1	cup boiling water
6	whole cloves	2	tablespoons salt
2	lemons sliced		

Thaw the venison, if frozen. Rinse well and place in deep non-corrosive casserole. Mix together marinade ingredients and pour over the venison. Turn to coat. Cover and marinate 3 days, or at least 48 hours. Turn twice a day. Never pierce the meat when turning.

Remove venison from marinade and pat dry. Heat oil in large, heavy skillet or pot that will hold the meat and marinade. Brown venison well on both sides. Add marinade mixture, heat to boiling, reduce heat and cover. Cook at a bubbly simmer until venison is tender, about 45 minutes to an hour. Check, turning the meat, and when it is fork tender, it is done.

Remove meat and onions. Strain the liquid and add enough water to make 2 cups. This is important, otherwise the gravy can be too tangy. Pour liquid back into skillet or pot, cover and bring to a boil. Add the crushed ginger snaps, a little at a time, stirring well with a whisk. When thick enough, don't add anymore. Serve the venison sliced with the onions and gravy.

If you are not serving right away, leave the venison in the gravy, so it doesn't dry out. Good with mashed potatoes or spaetzle.

Venison Shepherd's Pie

Makes 4-6 servings

1 diced carrot	½ cup Tony Chachere Instant
1 diced celery stalk	Roux Mix
1½ lbs. ground venison	no-stick cooking spray
1 medium onion, chopped	½ teaspoon dried oregano
2 cloves garlic, minced	½ teaspoon ground thyme
¼ cup red wine	½ cup seasoned Italian
½ cup peas, fresh or frozen	breadcrumbs
2 cups mashed potatoes	1 teaspoon Old Bay seasoning

Gravy:
  cooking liquid from carrots
  and celery
  cold water to make 2 cups

Topping:
1 to 2 tablespoons wheat germ, or
  Italian breadcrumbs
  Dash of Old Bay

Preheat oven to 450°F.

Thaw venison, if frozen. Meanwhile, put the carrots in a small pot and cover with water. Boil a few minutes until starting to get soft. Add the celery and cook a little more. Do not overcook. Drain, reserving the liquid. Add a couple of ice cubes to cool liquid, then pour into a measuring cup and add enough water to make 2 cups. With a whisk, mix in the roux mix. When smooth, pour into pot and bring to a boil to thicken.

Spray a skillet with no-stick cooking spray. Add onion and sauté until beginning to soften. Add garlic and continue to sauté until beginning to get tinged with brown. Add the ground venison and cook until no longer pink. Add the red wine and reduce until almost gone. Pour in most of the gravy. Add Italian breadcrumbs to thicken the sauce so it isn't runny. Stir in the cooked carrots, celery, and peas.

Spray casserole with no-stick cooking spray. Spread meat filling evenly on the bottom. Pour over any leftover gravy made from the roux. Spread on the mashed potatoes, leaving a little texture. Sprinkle with wheat germ and Old Bay. Bake for 10 minutes at 450°, then run under broiler for 2-3 minutes, to lightly brown the top.

Good with a lettuce and raw vegetable salad and whole-wheat bread.

Large Game

Black Bear Enchiladas with Ranchero Sauce

Makes 8 servings

2	pounds black bear or other game. If black bear is not available, wild boar is a good substitute.
1	large onion, sliced
3	cloves garlic, chopped
2	tablespoons red wine vinegar
2	cups beef stock

1	16-ounce can crushed tomatoes
2	tablespoons chili powder
3	whole red and/or green bell peppers, diced
2	tablespoons olive oil
8	10-inch corn tortillas, warmed
1	cup Monterey Jack, shredded

In a casserole dish or Dutch oven, bring the meat to a boil with the onion, garlic, vinegar and beef stock. Cover and simmer over a low heat for 2 to 3 hours. After the first hour, add the crushed tomatoes and chili powder. They should simmer with the meat for a minimum of 45 minutes. When the meat is very, very, tender, remove it with a slotted spoon and shred it on a plate. When all the meat is shredded, return it to the stock. Meanwhile, sauté the bell peppers in the olive oil until very tender. Add peppers to meat, and heat uncovered until almost all liquid is evaporated. Preheat oven to 400°. Soften corn tortillas by dipping into hot water before filling. Place about ½ cup of mixture in center of corn tortilla, roll into small bundles, place seam side down in greased casserole dish and cover with ranchero sauce and grated cheese. Bake at 400° until lightly browned. Serve with additional heated Ranchero Sauce on the side.

Ranchero Sauce

Makes 2¹/₂ cups

2   cups tomatoes, chopped
¼   cup water
1   tablespoon onions, chopped
1   tablespoon garlic, crushed
½   teaspoon salt

¼   teaspoon pepper
¼   teaspoon sugar
¼   teaspoon ground cumin
⅓   cup cilantro, chopped

Cook the tomatoes and water uncovered over medium heat until tomatoes soften. Mash tomatoes, add onions, garlic and spices and stir until well blended. Remove any tomato skins. Just before serving, add the cilantro. Serve warm over burritos. Makes about 2½ cups.

Bear Pot Roast

Makes 8 servings

5	pounds bear rump roast	2	tablespoons Champagne
1	garlic clove		vinegar
	salt and pepper to taste	2	parsnips, diced
	flour or cornmeal	2	potatoes, diced
	(optional)	3	carrots, diced
1	tablespoon butter	4	celery stalks, diced
1	tablespoon vegetable oil		red wine or water

Preheat oven to 325°. Rinse the bear rump roast, pat dry and rub with garlic, salt and pepper. Sprinkle with flour or cornmeal if you like a darker crust. Heat the butter and oil in a Dutch oven or cast iron skillet. Sear the meat well on all sides. Just before putting roast in oven, add vinegar and turn to coat. Cover tightly and bake for approximately 3 hours, or 35 to 45 minutes per pound. If pot becomes dry, add red wine or water, as needed, and baste frequently. During the last hour of roasting add the diced parsnips, potatoes, carrots, and celery stalks to the meat. When done, remove from Dutch oven. To make gravy, loosen pan drippings, add flour, mixed with a little water and simmer until thickened. Add salt and pepper to taste.

Boar Chop Casserole

Makes 4 servings

4	boar chops	1	8-ounce can cream of	
	flour		mushroom soup	
	salt & pepper to taste	1	cup milk	
1	tablespoon blackening	1	cup fresh green beans,	
	seasoning		trimmed	
1	large potato, sliced	1	cup fresh button	
2	large onions, sliced		mushrooms, sliced	

Preheat oven to 375°.

Grease a large baking dish. In plastic bag, put flour, salt, pepper and blackening seasoning and shake well to mix. Place 1 boar chop at a time in bag, shake to coat well, repeat with remaining 3 chops. Place a single layer on the bottom of casserole dish. Place the thinly sliced raw potato over chops, then the onion slices. Sprinkle with a little additional dry dredging mixture. In a small mixing bowl, mix the cream of mushroom soup and milk and stir well, adding additional milk if too thick. Pour over chops with potato and onions. Cover the dish with foil.

Bake slowly for 1 hour. Uncover and add the green beans and mushrooms. Replace cover and return to oven for ½ to 1 hour, until chops are completely tender. Great with baked apples or applesauce.

Wild Boar Chops with Blueberry Pecan Relish

Makes 6 servings

6   boar chops, 1½-inches
thick
ground black pepper

orange juice
butter to grease casserole

Preheat oven to 350°. Heat a heavy skillet over medium-high heat. Pan-sear chops slowly, turning to brown. Season with salt and pepper. Remove and place in buttered casserole, in a single layer. Cover each chop with a little Blueberry Pecan Relish. Bake covered at 350° for 1½ hours, or until very tender. Remove cover and continued to bake 10-15 minutes, to brown. Add a bit of orange juice, if needed near the end of baking time, so that the chops do not dry out.

Blueberry Pecan Relish

Makes 3½ cups

1   orange
½ lemon
½ lime
¼ cup granulated sugar

1   pint fresh or frozen
blueberries
½ cup pecans, chopped
1   tablespoon brandy or cognac

Quarter and seed the orange, lemon, and lime keeping the peels on. Place citrus fruit and sugar in food processor and process with on/off turns to coarsely chop, but not puree. Add the blueberries and quickly process again with a few on/off turns to make a relish. Place fruit mixture in bowl; add chopped pecans and cognac. Stir well, and refrigerate at least 1 hour before serving to allow flavors to blend. Remember, this is a relish, not a sauce!

Stuffed Boar Roulades with Pecan Gravy

Makes 8 servings

2	cups cornbread stuffing crumbs		flour for dredging
⅔	cup milk or light cream	2	tablespoons butter
2	eggs, slightly beaten	2	tablespoons vegetable oil
2	teaspoons water	¾	cup Southern Comfort
½	cup butter, melted	2	cups chicken stock
1½	cups pecans, finely chopped	2	cups heavy cream
1	4-pound boneless boar roast	2	tablespoons cornstarch
	freshly ground black pepper		dissolved in a little water

Combine cornbread stuffing crumbs, milk, the beaten egg plus water, the melted butter and 1 cup of the finely chopped pecans. Mix well so all the crumbs absorb the liquids, and let stand for about ½ hour. This should not be a mushy stuffing.

Meanwhile, slice boar meat thin enough, ¼-inch to ½-inch thick, to roll around stuffing. Season boar with black pepper and dredge in flour. In a large skillet, heat the remaining butter and oil and brown the boar on all sides. Cool and then spread a little stuffing on each piece of sliced boar and roll up. Tie with string. Place the boar roulades in a buttered casserole large enough to accommodate them. Preheat oven to 350°.

In the skillet in which you browned the boar, pour ½ cup Southern Comfort, turn up the heat and reduce the liquor by half, scraping up any bits from the bottom of the pan. Add the chicken stock and stir. Pour some of this mixture into the casserole, just enough to cover the bottom. Bake the roulades about 45 minutes on one side and then turn over and bake on the other side for about 30 to 45 minutes, or until fork tender. Make gravy by straining juices from baking pan into skillet with remaining chicken stock mixture. Add the heavy cream, stir to blend and simmer about 5 minutes. Add the cornstarch and water mixture a little at a time, the rest of the pecans and the remaining ¼ cup Southern Comfort. Simmer another 10 minutes, stirring constantly until the gravy thickens and the flavors blend. Serve over the Boar Roulades.

Southwestern Wild Boar Stew

Makes 6 to 8 servings

4   pounds boneless wild boar, cubed
3   tablespoons vegetable oil
3   large onions, diced
1   cup corn kernels
    cilantro for garnish

Marinade:

3   bay leaves
2   poblano peppers, finely diced
8   cloves garlic, minced
3   cups V-8® vegetable juice
¼   cup balsamic vinegar
¼   cup Worcestershire sauce
3   tablespoons sun-dried tomatoes, chopped
4   chipotle peppers in adobo sauce
2   tablespoons chili powder
1   tablespoon ground cumin
¼   cup brown sugar
1   tablespoon ground sage
3   tablespoons salt
½   cup fresh cilantro, chopped and blanched

Combine all marinade ingredients in a large bowl and mix well. Add the cubed boar meat, turning to cover well. Cover and marinate in refrigerator for at least 24 hours.

Heat the oil in a large pot over medium heat. Add the onions and sauté, slowly, for about ½ hour, until the onions are brown and caramelized. Add the marinated meat and marinade liquid to the onions and stir to blend thoroughly. Cover the pot and simmer over low heat 2 to 2½ hours, or until the meat is tender. Stir occasionally.

When tender, pour in corn and continue to simmer 15 minutes. Serve hot and garnish with additional fresh cilantro.

Buffalo Steaks Smothered with Onions

Makes 4 servings

1½ cups yellow onions, sliced
1 tablespoon butter
2 teaspoons olive oil, plus extra
for brushing
1 teaspoon fresh rosemary, chopped

2 tablespoons fresh cilantro,
chopped
salt and black pepper to taste
4 10-ounce buffalo steaks

Preheat the grill or broiler. Heat the butter and olive oil in a skillet and sauté the onions for 3 to 4 minutes; add fresh rosemary and continue to sauté until tender. Add the cilantro, season with salt and pepper and hold, keeping it warm.

Rub the meat with salt and pepper. Lightly brush each side with olive oil. Grill the steaks over medium hot fire for 4 to 5 minutes a side, or until the steaks are cooked on the outside and medium rare on the inside. Put the steaks on a warm platter, or individual heated plates and top each steak with some of the onion mixture.

Buffalo Pot Pie

Makes 8 servings

4 pounds buffalo meat
¾ cup bacon, diced
2 cups onion, chopped
½ cup carrots, diced
2 cloves garlic, chopped
½ cup green peas, frozen or
fresh
1 cup quick-cooking barley

⅓ cup brown gravy (demi-
glace), canned or packaged
3 tablespoons marjoram
3 tablespoons thyme
salt to taste
1 tablespoon white pepper
10 ounces pie dough
egg wash

Chop buffalo meat in very small cubes or grind. Heat bacon in large skillet, add meat, onion, carrots, and salt. When meat is nearly cooked add garlic and peas, stirring well. While meat is cooking, preheat the oven to 425° and cook the barley in 3 to 4 cups water with salt to taste and drain. Add barley, demi-glace, herbs, salt and pepper to meat mixture. Taste to adjust flavorings. Cool to room temperature. Pour into individual pie dishes or one large round casserole. Cover with pie dough, brush with egg wash—a mixture of beaten egg and a little salt. Bake in preheated oven until crust is nicely browned and crisp.

Buffalo Burgers with Chipotle Mayonnaise

Makes 4 servings

1	tablespoon olive oil	½	teaspoon black pepper
3	cups sweet yellow onions	½	teaspoon garlic powder
1½	pounds extra lean ground buffalo	2	tablespoons Worcestershire sauce
1	teaspoon ground cumin	4	onion hamburger buns
½	teaspoon salt		

Preheat the grill or broiler.

Heat the olive oil and sauté onions until they are soft and golden brown. Set aside.

Make the chipotle mayonnaise (recipe below).

Using your hands, thoroughly mix the seasonings into the ground meat and form 4 patties ½-inch thick. Grill the burgers over medium hot fire for about 5 minutes on each side. Put the buns on the grill and lightly toast. Serve the burgers on the buns, topped with warm sautéed onions and chipotle mayonnaise.

Chipotle Mayonnaise

Makes 1¹/₂ cups

1	cup mayonnaise
6	ounces chipotle peppers canned in adobo sauce

Puree canned chipotles in adobo sauce, add 1 cup of mayonnaise, stir well. Store in the refrigerator in a covered jar or container until needed. (You can store Chipotle Mayonnaise up to a week.)

Wild Game Birds

Indian Curried Doves

Makes 4 servings

8	doves, cleaned and dressed	2	garlic cloves
1½	cups whole grain mustard	2	1-inch pieces fresh ginger,
1	cup olive oil, divided		chopped
	salt and pepper to taste	2	tablespoons curry powder
1	tablespoon wine vinegar	1	cup canned tomatoes
1	tablespoon butter	2	cups chicken stock
½	cup white onions, chopped		salt and pepper
½	cup red bell pepper, chopped		chives, chopped, for garnish

Marinate the doves for 3 hours refrigerated, in a mixture of mustard, ½ cup olive oil, salt and pepper and vinegar. Turn the birds often so they are well coated. Heat the remaining olive oil and butter in a heavy skillet and sauté the doves until they are brown. Remove them to a medium pot. To the pan, add the onions, red bell pepper, garlic and ginger and sauté until brown. Stir in the curry powder, blending well. Add the tomatoes and chicken stock; bring to a boil. Remove from heat and scrape into the pot containing the doves. Stir well, season with salt and pepper to taste. Cover and simmer slowly until the birds are tender, about 1½ hours. Serve doves over rice and garnish with chopped chives.

Dove Amandine

Makes 4 to 6 servings

8	doves, cleaned and dressed	½	cup butter, melted
	black pepper	3	cups cooked wild rice
	salt		(optional accompaniment)
	fresh or dried sage		parsley, for garnish
4	bacon slices, halved		

Preheat oven to 350°. Split each dove in half lengthwise. Season with pepper, salt and sage. Place bone side down in a roasting pan, cover with bacon slices, held in place with skewers or toothpicks. Roast in oven until tender, approximately 1 hour basting frequently with the melted butter and pan juices. Remove dove from juices, place dove over wild rice. Combine almond lemon butter. With a spoon lift most of the almonds out and place over doves, then brush with Almond Lemon Butter and drizzle with pan juices if desired. Garnish with fresh parsley.

Almond Lemon Butter:
½ cup butter melted
2 tablespoons lemon juice
½ cup toasted, slivered almonds

Bourbon Marinated Grilled Doves

Makes 4 servings

8   dove breasts, skin on

Marinade:

½   cup bourbon or whiskey
½   cup soy sauce
½   cup maple syrup
2   tablespoons blackstrap
      molasses
¼   cup brown sugar
2   tablespoons garlic chili sauce
      or chipotle hot sauce

2   tablespoons garlic, chopped
2   tablespoons mild fresh herbs:
      equal parts tarragon, parsley,
      and chopped marjoram
½   cup olive oil
2   cups water
⅓   cup rice wine vinegar

Combine marinade ingredients and add dove breasts. Turn to coat well. Cover and marinate in refrigerator, for at least 3 hours. Turn gas grill on high and preheat for 20 minutes, or build a hot charcoal fire. Take dove breasts out of marinade and place on hot grill. Grill 2 minutes on each side or until done. Serve immediately. Pecan cornbread stuffing is a nice accompaniment to this dish. (Note: recipe can also be used with quail.)

Black Tea-Lacquered Duck

Makes 8 servings

8	duck breasts, skin on	1	tablespoon oil, to season
½	cup black tea leaves, finely ground		skillet

Remove duck from Black Tea-Lacquered Duck Marinade (recipe below) and allow to drain on racks. (Save marinade.) Pat duck breasts dry. Dust with black tea. Allow to stand 1 hour. Preheat oven to 350°.

Heat a cast iron skillet or other suitable pan, wiped with oil, to crackling stage—extremely hot, hot, hot! Place duck breasts in skillet, skin side down. They should really crackle. Caramelize (but do not burn) the skin. Turn over and cook duck breasts approximately 3 to 4 minutes. Remove duck from skillet and place in roasting pan to finish in a 350° oven for 15 to 20 minutes.

Strain reserved marinade. Bring to a boil to remove any impurities and thicken with cornstarch or arrowroot. Slice duck breast to fan and serve on a bed of fried rice or sautéed apples. Drizzle with sauce.

Black Tea-Lacquered Duck Marinade

Makes 8 servings

2	cups chicken stock	1	tablespoon black pepper
¾	cup honey	1	teaspoon red pepper flakes, crushed
½	cup orange marmalade		
1¼	cups ketchup	2	tablespoons fresh ginger, minced
3	cloves garlic, crushed		
1	cup soy sauce	2	bay leaves

Mix all ingredients for marinade and heat to simmer. Remove from heat and allow to cool. Pour over duck breasts. Cover and refrigerate for 24 hours.

Breast of Duck with Grapes

Makes 8 servings

8   6-ounce wild duck breasts
8   cloves garlic, peeled and
    chopped
1½ tablespoons soy sauce
⅔   cup olive oil
1 to 2 sticks of butter
    salt and pepper
¾   cup flour
⅔   cup shallots, chopped

⅔   pound fresh mushrooms,
    quartered
3   10-ounce cans cream of
    mushroom soup, condensed
⅔   cup dry sherry
1½ cups heavy cream
½   pound green grapes,
    cut in halves
½   cup slivered almonds,
    toasted

Place the duck breasts in a ceramic dish. Marinate the duck breasts with the garlic, soy sauce, and olive oil, overnight if possible.

Remove breasts from marinade. Melt 1 stick butter in a heavy skillet. Season the duck with salt and pepper, dip in flour, and sauté over low heat until light brown. Remove from skillet and place duck on a heated platter. Add more butter to the pan, if necessary, and add the shallots and simmer until soft. Add the fresh mushrooms, mushroom soup, sherry, heavy cream, and grapes and bring to a boil. Cook a few minutes, until lightly thickened and mushrooms are softened. Ladle over the duck breasts, and garnish with toasted almonds.

Serve with fettuccine.

Wild Duck with Champagne Peach Sauce

Makes 8 servings

4	pounds wild duck breast or whole wild duck	⅓	cup brown sugar
1½	cans peach halves in water, sliced and drained	½	teaspoon nutmeg
½	cup Champagne	½	teaspoon cinnamon
		½	cup pecan pieces, toasted (optional)

Prepare the wild duck by braising in liquid, or grill wild duck breasts. Serve with Champagne Peach Sauce.

Drain peaches. Reserve four peach halves for garnish. Puree remaining peaches in blender. Add Champagne, very carefully with lid on blender, give puree button one quick on/off spin to combine Champagne and peaches.

Transfer mixture to small saucepan. Add brown sugar, nutmeg and cinnamon and stir until completely blended, over high heat bring to a boil. Reduce heat and simmer for 10 minutes.

Serve sauce hot over whole braised duck or grilled duck breast. Garnish with peach halves and optional toasted pecan pieces.

Tumbleweed Duck Breasts with Orange Sauce

Makes 8 servings

4   large ducks
2   cups your favorite cornbread stuffing, prepared

⅓   cup mandarin orange segments
½   cup orange juice, as needed
    toothpicks

Duck broth for Orange Sauce (page 67) should be made 1 to 2 days in advance. Make the Orange Sauce before grilling the duck breasts.

Cut the breasts away from the duck. Wrap the breasts well in plastic wrap and refrigerate until ready to cook. Reserve legs and carcasses to make the broth. Cover legs and carcasses with water. Add salt, bring to a boil, then reduce heat and simmer 2 to 3 hours, skimming occasionally. Reserve meat and save for other uses. Discard bones. Strain the broth through cheesecloth. Reserve 8 cups.

Preheat oven to 400°. Prepare cornbread stuffing, adding mandarin orange segments and orange juice to make it fairly wet. With spoon, divide stuffing mixture in to 8 portions. Remove duck breasts from plastic, season with salt and pepper and place, skin side down, on cutting board. Spread a portion of the stuffing mixture in center of each breast. Wrap breast meat around the stuffing, and secure with toothpicks. Place stuffed duck breasts in greased oven-proof casserole. Cover and bake for about 20 minutes, or until duck is tender. Remove toothpicks and serve with Orange Sauce.

Orange Sauce

Makes 3 cups

8	cups duck broth	¼	cup cider vinegar
1	tablespoon cornstarch	¼	cup orange juice
2	tablespoons cold water	1	tablespoon mandarin
⅓	cup mandarin orange		orange jam, or orange
	segments, cut in half		marmalade
¼	cup brandy or Cognac		salt and freshly ground
½	cup sugar		pepper to taste

Place the broth in a large saucepan and simmer over medium heat until reduced to 2½ cups. Combine the cornstarch and cold water in a small bowl and mix well. Add this mixture to the reduced broth, whisking constantly. Simmer 1 to 2 minutes, or until the broth is thickened. Set aside and keep warm. Combine the mandarin orange segments with the brandy, set aside. Combine the sugar and 1 teaspoon of the orange juice in a medium sauté pan and cook over medium heat without stirring. Once the sugar has begun to melt, stir occasionally until the sugar is completely melted and golden brown, about 8 minutes. Immediately add the vinegar and continue to cook until reduced by half. Add the remaining orange juice to the reduced sugar, drain the brandy from the oranges and add it to the orange juice mixture. Simmer until reduced by half. Add to the thickened broth with mandarin orange pieces and preserves. Blend, adding the salt and pepper to taste. Set sauce aside and keep warm while cooking duck breasts. Spoon some sauce over the duck breasts before serving. Pass remaining warm sauce at the table.

Wild Duck Casserole

Makes 8 servings

1½ pounds wild duck meat or 2 wild ducks
  duck or chicken stock, to cover
1 cup wild rice
2 tablespoons butter
  salt and pepper to taste
1 pound mushrooms, sautéed
1 onion, minced
2 celery stalks, finely chopped
1 green pepper, diced
¼ cup bacon, cooked, crumbled
  breadcrumbs
  pimento strips or chopped parsley for garnish

Cut up the duck and cover with stock. Simmer until tender. Remove meat and cut into large dice. Boil wild rice in remaining duck stock until half cooked, about 15 to 20 minutes. Preheat oven to 350°. Butter a casserole dish. Combine rice, duck, vegetables, bacon, adding a small amount of stock, about one cup, to finish cooking the rice. Sprinkle top with breadcrumbs. Cover and bake for ½ hour. Garnish with pimento strips or chopped parsley.

Game Bird Wellington

Makes 4 servings

2	tablespoons butter	1	tablespoon parsley, snipped
⅓	cup mushrooms, chopped		
2	tablespoons green onion, diced	2	whole duck or pheasant breasts, boneless, skinned and split into four pieces
1	tablespoons brandy or Cognac	1	sheet frozen puff pastry
4	ounces liverwurst	1	large egg, beaten with
		1	tablespoon water

Heat oven to 375°. In non-stick skillet, melt 1 tablespoon butter over medium heat. Add mushrooms, onions and brandy. Cook 2 to 4 minutes, or until onions are tender. In small mixing bowl, combine mushroom mixture, liverwurst and parsley. Set aside.

In same skillet, melt remaining 1 tablespoon butter over medium heat. Add breast halves. Cook for 8 to 10 minutes, turning until meat is browned. Remove from heat and keep warm.

On lightly floured surface, roll pastry sheet to 14-inch square. Cut sheet into 4 individual 7-inch squares. Place 1 breast half on each square. Spread liverwurst mixture evenly over top of breast halves. Brush inside edges of pastry with the beaten egg and water mixture. Bring the two sides of the pastry together, closing the pastry completely around the breasts. Pinch edges and the ends to seal. Place on ungreased baking sheet. Bake 20 to 25 minutes, or until golden brown.

Serve with Sherry Wine Sauce (see Page 70).

Sherry Wine Sauce

Makes 6 cups

¾   cup bacon fat
3   tablespoons olive oil
3   tablespoons butter
1½ cups carrots,peeled and
    diced
1½ cups onion, diced
1   cup leeks, diced
½   cup celery, sliced
1   head garlic, cut in half
    crosswise with skin

1   cup sherry wine vinegar
1   cup sherry wine
3   cups chicken stock
12 black peppercorns
¼   cup cumin seeds, roasted
2   dried ancho chili peppers,
    toasted and seeded
2   dried chipotle chili peppers,
    toasted and seeded
1   bay leaf, crushed

In a medium saucepan, on medium heat add together the bacon fat, oil and butter. Cook 3 to 5 minutes, or until browned. Add carrot, onion, leeks, celery and garlic and cook until vegetables are softened. Add vinegar and wine, reduce to half. Add stock, peppercorns, cumin seeds, chili peppers and bay leaf. Reduce to half again until you have a light sauce. Strain and reserve. If a thicker sauce is desired, mix a little cornstarch and water together, add and bring to a boil to thicken. Serve with Game Bird Wellington. Extra sauce keeps several days in refrigerator or may be frozen.

Honey and Chili Glazed Quail

Makes 6 servings

6   quail (See glaze recipe.)

Preheat oven to 450°. Grill glazed quail, skin side down over hot charcoal or preheated gas grill until marked. Remove quail and finish in hot oven for 5 to 7 minutes, while frequently brushing with glaze. Remove quail to heated platter and spoon sauce over and around quail.

Honey and Chili Glaze

Makes 6 servings

2	tablespoons olive oil	3	tablespoons sherry wine vinegar
6	cloves garlic, chopped		
1	poblano chili, seeded, deveined and julienned	½	cup honey
			salt and pepper to taste
1	ancho chili, toasted in a dry skillet, soaked in water to soften, drained and then rough chopped (remove seeds, if you don't like it hot)		

Heat oil, add garlic and peppers and sauté for 3 minutes. Add vinegar and reduce by half. Add honey. Remove from heat, allow to steep. Strain, season to taste and cool. Brush on quail before grilling.

Grilled Quail Salad with Mango

Makes 4 servings

8 quail breasts, skinless, marinated overnight

2 heads butter lettuce or ½ pound mesclun mix

1 large papaya

3 large ripe mangos

½ medium pineapple, peeled and in chunks

1 red onion, sliced thin walnuts, pine nuts, for garnish, optional

Marinate the quail overnight in Quail Marinade. Grill it over charcoal or a preheated gas grill until the flesh is pale pink inside. Baste with marinade while grilling, taking care not to overcook the quail. Wash and dry the lettuce leaves or mesclun mix. Peel and seed the papaya, cut it in half lengthwise, and slice each papaya in half vertically into about 10 pieces. Place a little lettuce or mesclun mix on each plate and fan out 3 slices of papaya. Peel the mangos and pineapple and cut into chunks. Place mango and pineapple chunks on one side of the fan. Add a few slices of onion. Cut the grilled quail breasts into medallions and fan opposite the papaya. Dress the salad with your favorite fruit or citrus vinaigrette. If desired, garnish with walnuts or pine nuts.

Quail Marinade

Makes 4 servings

¼ cup olive oil

2 garlic cloves, minced

2 tablespoons white wine

2 tablespoons soy sauce

2 tablespoons fresh ginger, minced

Blend all ingredients.

Quail Roasted in Polenta

Makes 12 servings

12   6 to 8-ounce quail, necks removed
2   tablespoons Italian seasoning
2   tablespoons olive oil

1   large garlic clove, chopped
hot cooked polenta
fresh rosemary or thyme sprigs for garnish

Preheat the oven to 425°. Grease a large oven-to-table baking dish and set aside. Rub the quail with Italian seasoning. In a large skillet, heat the oil and garlic over medium high heat. Add the quail and brown on all sides. Remove pan from heat and let quail cool, until they can be handled. This can be done in advance. Reheat quail before completing the dish.

Mound the hot polenta in the center of a large warm serving platter. Arrange the cooked quail, in a circle, standing upright in the polenta, breast meat facing out. Gently push the quail down into the polenta until they can stand. Bake for 12 to 15 minutes, or until quail are tender. Garnish platter with sprigs of rosemary or thyme.

Polenta

Makes 4 servings

4   cups chicken broth
½   teaspoon coarse salt, optional
½   cup cornmeal
½   cup semolina

½   cup parmesan cheese, freshly grated
2   tablespoons unsalted butter

Heat the chicken stock and optional salt in a 2-quart saucepan over medium heat until almost boiling. Reduce the heat to simmer, mix together the cornmeal and semolina, and slowly stir in into the hot stock, stirring constantly with a wire whisk. To avoid lumps, continue stirring until all the polenta has been added and the mixture begins to thicken, 20 to 25 minutes. Remove from the heat. Stir in the cheese and butter and season with salt as needed. Immediately pour into baking dish. Complete recipe with quail. Instant polentas are also available in most grocery stores.

Quail Stuffed with Apricot and Raisins

Makes 4 servings

8   whole quail, dressed
     salt and pepper

1   cup orange juice for basting
     Raisin-Apricot Sauce

Stuffing Ingredients:

⅓   cup orange juice
1½   cups fresh breadcrumbs
½   cup plump raisins, chopped
4   tablespoons apricots, diced
1   egg, lightly beaten

½   tablespoon cinnamon
½   teaspoon thyme
½   tablespoon ground cloves
½   cup unsalted butter, cut in
     chunks

Combine stuffing ingredients. The mixture should be slightly wet. Add additional drops of orange juice, if necessary. Stuff the birds and truss legs.

Preheat oven to 450°. Sprinkle birds with salt and pepper. Place in shallow greased roasting pan and bake in preheated oven for 20 minutes, basting frequently with orange juice. Glaze with Raisin-Apricot Sauce. Serve hot.

Raisin Apricot Sauce

Makes 1½ cups

1   10-ounce jar apricot jam
½   cup water
¼   cup butter

1   teaspoon cinnamon
1   teaspoon ground cloves
½   cup raisins

In a small saucepan combine jam with water, stir over low heat until well combined, add butter, cinnamon, cloves, raisins. Cook until butter is melted and sauce begins to bubble. In blender puree mixture and glaze quail.

Quail with Crawfish and Wild Mushrooms

Makes 4 servings

8 slices bacon, cut into 1-inch pieces	1½ cups chicken broth
¼ cup flour	8 quail, breastbone removed and split down back
1 cup canned tomatoes, chopped	1 teaspoon salt
1 cup onions, chopped	½ teaspoon cayenne pepper
1 tablespoon garlic, chopped	¼ teaspoon ground black pepper
1 cup crawfish tail meat	¼ cup lemon juice
2 cups sliced mushrooms (shiitake, oyster, portobello)	2 tablespoons cilantro or parsley, chopped
½ cup dry sherry	

Fry the bacon in a large skillet over medium heat until crisp. Remove bacon from skillet and set aside on paper towels, leaving about ¼ cup fat in the skillet. Add the flour to the fat and make a medium brown roux by stirring constantly over medium heat for 8 to 10 minutes more. Add the tomatoes, onions, garlic, crawfish, mushrooms, sherry and broth and bring to a boil. Add the quail, salt, cayenne and black pepper and simmer for about 30 minutes, basting and turning quail every 8 to 10 minutes. Stir in lemon juice and cilantro or parsley. Garnish with reserved cooked bacon pieces. Serve with rice.

Stuffed Quail or Dove with Braised Bavarian Cabbage

Makes 8 servings

8	whole quail or doves salt and pepper	1	cup apple juice for basting

Apple-Raisin Stuffing:

1½	cups fresh breadcrumbs	⅓	cup apple juice
½	cup apples, cubed	1	whole egg, lightly beaten
½	cup raisins, plumped and chopped	½	teaspoon dried thyme
		½	teaspoon ground cloves

Braised Bavarian Cabbage:

2	pounds red cabbage	6	slices bacon, cut into matchsticks
2	carrots, shredded		
½	large yellow onion, chopped fine	2	Granny Smith apples, peeled and sliced thin
1	tablespoon butter	½	cup apple cider vinegar
½	cup stock or water	1	tablespoon sugar

Preheat oven to 450°. Combine stuffing ingredients. The mixture should be slightly wet. Stuff the birds and truss legs. Sprinkle birds with salt and pepper. Place in shallow roasting pan and bake in preheated oven for 15 to 20 minutes, basting frequently with apple juice. Keep warm.

Quarter the cabbage. Remove core and finely shred the cabbage. In heavy skillet, sauté the carrots and onions in butter. Deglaze pan with stock or water. In separate pan, cook bacon pieces until crisp. Add bacon to carrots and onions and stir. Fold in shredded cabbage, Granny Smith apples, apple cider vinegar and sugar. Cover and cook gently for 15 to 20 minutes, stirring occasionally, until cabbage is crisp tender and apples are cooked.

To serve:
Place Bavarian Cabbage on center of plate. Put quail or dove on top and untruss. If desired, drizzle additional warmed apple juice over top.

Pheasant with Cherries and Walnuts

Makes 8 servings

4	2-pound pheasants	8	ounces fresh mushrooms
8	cloves garlic, peeled and chopped	⅔	cup dry sherry
1½	tablespoons soy sauce	1⅓	cups heavy cream
⅔	cup olive oil	½	pound cherries, pitted and halved
¼	pound butter		
	salt and pepper	½	cup mandarin orange segments, sliced
¾	cup flour		
¾	cup shallots, chopped	¾	cup walnut pieces, lightly toasted
3	10-ounce cans cream of mushroom soup, condensed		

Step One: Preparation of the Pheasant—
With a sharp knife remove the two breasts from the center bone and also all the meat from the legs. Remove all the skin and excess fat. Place the pheasant breast and legs in a ceramic dish Reserve the bones for stock. Marinate with the garlic, soy sauce, and olive oil, overnight if possible.

Step Two: Preparation of the Dish—
Melt the butter in a heavy skillet, season the pheasant with salt and pepper, dip in flour, and sauté over low heat until light brown and cooked through. Remove from skillet and place pheasant on a heated platter. Add more butter to the pan, if necessary, and add the shallots and simmer until soft. Add the mushroom soup, fresh mushrooms, sherry wine, heavy cream, cherries and oranges; bring to a boil. Garnish with walnuts and ladle over the pheasant.

Pheasant, Wild Rice and Black Bean Casserole

Makes 6 servings

1 medium stewing pheasant	1 green pepper, diced
1½ quarts game bird or chicken stock	1 red pepper, diced
1 cup wild rice	½ cup cooked black beans
½ pound sautéed mushrooms	salt and pepper
2 stalks celery, finely diced	1 dash cayenne (optional)
1 onion, minced	¼ cup cilantro, chopped

Cut up pheasant and cover with stock, simmer until tender. Remove skin and bones. Cut meat into large dice. Boil wild rice in the stock the pheasant was cooked in, until rice is half done, about 20 minutes. In buttered casserole dish, combine rice, pheasant chunks, vegetables, seasonings and beans adding small amount of stock to finish cooking rice. Cover casserole and bake at 350° for ½ hour. Garnish with fresh cilantro.

Pheasant Cordon Bleu

Makes 4 servings

2 boned pheasant breasts, cut in half	salt and pepper
4 slices prosciutto or smoked ham	¾ cup flour
4 slices Monterey Jack cheese	2 eggs, beaten
	1½ cups fine breadcrumbs
	vegetable oil for frying

Place 4 half breasts under wax paper and flatten them with a mallet to ½-inch thickness. Place each ½ breast on a platter and put a piece of prosciutto or smoked ham and then a piece of Monterey Jack cheese on top. Roll each filet up jelly roll style and secure with toothpicks. Place in refrigerator for 2 hours. Remove rolls from refrigerator. Dip each piece

(Continued on next page)

Pheasant Cordon Bleu *(Continued from previous page)*

into flour, then into beaten eggs, then roll in breadcrumbs so it is completely coated. Fasten ends with additional toothpicks if needed. Heat oil in fryer or deep skillet, until hot, 360°. Pheasant rolls should be completely immersed in the oil and fried until a deep golden brown. Remove the rolls, drain on paper towels and serve hot. If you do not have a fryer, you may pan fry the top and bottom of the rolls, then finish in a 400° oven for 15 minutes. An Alfredo sauce drizzled over the top is a nice accompaniment.

Smoked Pheasant and Toasted Walnut Salad

Makes 2 servings

1 ¾ cups smoked pheasant (duck or quail), skin and fat removed, diced

½ cup scallions with green stems, finely chopped

½ cup celery, finely diced

½ cup sweet red pepper, finely diced

½ cup chopped walnuts, toasted

½ cup mayonnaise

¼ cup orange juice

salt and pepper to taste

2 cups mesclun greens or your favorite lettuce

mandarin orange segments for garnish

Mix the pheasant, scallions, celery, red peppers and toasted walnuts in a bowl. In separate bowl whisk mayonnaise with orange juice. Add orange mayonnaise to pheasant mixture, season with salt and pepper. Blend well. Arrange lettuce on plates, scoop pheasant salad onto lettuce and garnish around scoop with mandarin orange segments. Duck or quail can also be substituted.

Blackened Goose with Apricot Fig Sauce

Makes 6 servings

1   boneless goose breast, split
2   goose thighs

Marinade:

1   cup red wine
1   teaspoon fresh sage, chopped
4   juniper berries, crushed
½   teaspoon finely chopped fresh
     rosemary

1   teaspoon minced garlic
2   tablespoons olive oil
1   tablespoon chili powder
2   tablespoons bacon drippings
2   teaspoons blackening
     seasoning

Combine ingredients for marinade, up to chili powder. Turn the goose pieces in the marinade, cover and let marinate overnight in the refrigerator. Rub off some, but not all the marinade. Preheat oven to 350°. Then rub on bacon drippings. Dust with blackening seasoning. Heat in iron skillet over high heat. Add the thighs, searing well on all sides. Remove from skillet, place thighs on a cookie sheet and bake for 30 minutes or until tender. When thighs are tender, add the breasts to a hot skillet. Sear breasts for 4 minutes on each side for a uniform sear without burning the spices. Place breasts on cookie sheet and bake 10 minutes or until done. Place blackened goose breasts and thighs on a bed of braised cabbage. Serve with apricot fig sauce (see page 150).

Little Critters

Roast Beaver

Makes 4-6 servings

2	young beavers	1	onion, sliced
½	cup dry orange peel	6	carrots
	salt	6	celery stalks, sliced
	ground black pepper		

Preheat oven to 450°. Remove tails from beavers, and strip all possible fat from the beaver meat. Season beavers with orange peel, salt and pepper. Place on a rack in a roaster. Place in oven and roast 15 to 20 minutes to sear the entire outside. Place onion slices over beavers and cover. Arrange carrots and celery around beavers on rack. Lower the heat to 350° and roast 30 minutes per pound. No basting is necessary. Carve into serving pieces.

Brunswick Stew

Makes 6 servings

5	pounds squirrel, skinned and disjointed	4	potatoes, peeled and diced
3	onions, sliced	2	quarts tomatoes, drained
6	pieces diced bacon, fried, and bacon fat reserved	½	teaspoon cayenne pepper
		4	teaspoons thyme
	salt and pepper to taste	2	cups fresh/frozen lima beans
2	quarts beef or game stock to cover	2	cups fresh/frozen corn
		2	cups fresh/frozen okra
			fine bread crumbs

Brown the squirrel meat and onions in hot bacon fat in a Dutch oven. Season with salt and pepper. Add stock to cover meat and simmer until tender. Remove the bones and any fat from the meat. Add the potatoes, tomatoes, reserved diced bacon, cayenne and thyme. Cook slowly for 45 minutes, then add the lima beans, corn and okra. Cook until vegetables are tender. Thicken with fine bread crumbs and adjust seasoning to taste before serving in heated bowls.

Baked Masala Squirrel

Makes 2 servings

2	squirrels cut in serving pieces	1	teaspoon paprika
		1	tablespoon flour
2	tablespoons ground West Indian Masala	½	teaspoon cinnamon
		½	cup bacon grease/oil
1	teaspoon ground black pepper	1	cup fine bread crumbs

Preheat oven to 375°. Dry the meat. Mix dry seasonings of West Indian Masala (page 95). Combine black pepper, paprika and flour. Season meat with Masala and seasoned flour. Dip in bacon grease to completely moisten, then dredge in fine bread crumbs. Arrange in baking dish. Bake 40 minutes on one side covered, turn and bake an additional 30 minutes uncovered. Should be well browned and very tender. Ground masala can be made (page 95) or purchased at your local specialty market.

Frog Leg Scampi

Makes 4 servings

10	pairs frog legs, split	2	tablespoons olive oil
	milk	6	cloves garlic, minced
	salt and pepper		chopped Italian parsley
	paprika		lemon slices
6	tablespoons unsalted butter		

Split frog legs, so they are no longer joined as a pair. Soak legs in milk in a shallow dish, overnight, or for at least 12 hours. Dry the legs and lightly season them with salt, pepper and paprika. In a heavy skillet, melt the butter, stir in the olive oil and when hot, brown the frog legs on both sides. Add the garlic and parsley. Cover and simmer, allowing the flavors to blend and the legs to cook through. Remove legs and place on a heated serving dish. Pour the butter/garlic mixture over the frog legs and top with lemon slices.

Squirrel Pot Pie

Makes 4 servings

Filling:

2½ cups cooked squirrel meat, cubed

2 cups potatoes, peeled, ¼-inch cubes

1½ cups frozen peas and carrots

1 10¾-ounce can cream of mushroom soup

½ cup celery, thinly sliced

½ cup onion, chopped

½ cup squirrel broth or chicken stock

½ teaspoon chicken bouillon

¼ teaspoon ground pepper

¼ teaspoon dried oregano

¼ teaspoon red pepper flakes

Crust:

¾ cup all-purpose flour

1 teaspoon baking powder

¼ teaspoon salt

¾ cup milk

½ cup butter, melted

Preheat oven to 375°. Spray 8-inch-square baking dish with cooking spray. Set aside. In a nonstick skillet, combine all filling ingredients. Bring to a boil over medium high heat. Remove from heat. Spoon filling into baking dish. Set aside.

In a medium mixing bowl, combine dry ingredients for crust. Add milk and butter. Stir with fork until dry ingredients are moistened. Spoon batter evenly over filling, spreading to edges. Bake 30 to 40 minutes, or until crust is golden brown.

Rabbit with Corn Dumplings

Makes 4 servings

2	rabbits, in parts, cleaned and dressed	1 1/2	quarts chicken broth
4	tablespoons butter	2	bay leaves
1 1/2	cups chopped onions	6	springs parsley
3	cloves garlic, minced	6	thyme leaves
4	tablespoons flour		pepper from mill
			parsley for garnish

If frozen, defrost rabbits, still wrapped, in cold water. Rinse pieces well, pat dry. Heat butter in <u>large</u> skillet and when foaming, add rabbit. Brown gently for about 10 minutes, until brown on all sides. If necessary, brown rabbit in batches. Reserve browned rabbit. Add onions to pan and cook 2 to 3 minutes, then add garlic and stir for a minute or two. Add flour and stir well. Then add broth and seasonings. Bring to a boil, reduce heat, and return rabbit to pan. Keep at a low simmering boil with cover askew to let a little steam escape. Cook about 1 hour, or until fork tender. When rabbit is tender add dumplings.

Dumplings

1 1/2	cups baking mix, e.g. Bisquick	1	cup corn kernels (these keep the dumplings from seeming heavy, and also keep them moist.)
2	teaspoons minced garlic		
1	teaspoon rubbed sage		
		2	tablespoons minced parsley
			Salt and pepper to taste

Blend dumpling ingredients in medium bowl. Spray insides of two soup spoons with no-stick. Using the two spoons, make egg-shaped dumplings from the dough. Carefully place on the gravy in the rabbit stew. Make sure they don't stick to the bottom of the pan. Cover pan and cook over medium-low for about 10 minutes, or until the dumplings swell, and a knife inserted comes out clean. Makes about 12-14 dumplings.

The rabbit is delicious served with turnip greens, seasoned with a little balsamic vinegar. At serving time, sprinkle rabbit and dumplings with additional parsley.

Rabbit Piquante

Makes 12 servings

3 medium rabbits (about 5 pounds)
½ cup flour
½ cup butter
2 large onions, diced
2 cups mushrooms, sliced
½ cup celery, diced
½ cup mixed bell peppers, diced
1 tablespoon garlic
¼ cup parsley
1 teaspoon thyme
2 teaspoons Tabasco® sauce
1 bay leaf
4 tablespoons blackening seasoning or to taste
8 ounces tomato sauce
1 cup white wine
3 cups chicken stock
½ cup green onions, sliced, for garnish

Cut each rabbit into 6 pieces. Dust rabbit with flour and brown in butter over medium high heat. Remove rabbit and add onions, mushrooms, celery, bell peppers and garlic. Cook until lightly brown. Add leftover dusting flour, stir well. Return rabbit to pot with seasonings and stir. Add tomato sauce and then the chicken stock, slowly incorporating it in small amounts. Simmer rabbit on low heat until tender. Sprinkle with green onions and serve.

Sweet and Sour Rabbit

Makes 4 servings

1	pound rabbit meat, boneless	¼	cup light brown sugar
2	tablespoons peanut oil	2	teaspoons fresh ginger,
1	cup green pepper, julienned		minced
1	tablespoon soy sauce	½	teaspoon dry mustard
½	cup onion, chopped	4	teaspoons cornstarch
1	tablespoon garlic, chopped	8	ounces pineapple chunks
3	tablespoons white wine	4	ounces water chestnuts
	vinegar	2	tablespoons chives, chopped
1	cup chicken broth		

In a wok or heavy skillet, heat 1 tablespoon peanut oil and lightly sauté the green pepper, soy sauce, onion and garlic; remove from pan and set aside. Wipe out pan. Add the remaining tablespoon of peanut oil and lightly brown rabbit, set aside. Make the sweet and sour sauce in the same pan, by pouring in the white wine vinegar, chicken broth, brown sugar, ginger and dry mustard. Stir and heat through. Dissolve cornstarch in a separate cup with a little bit of water. Add cornstarch mixture to sweet and sour sauce to thicken. Add the pineapple chunks and rabbit, cook 8 to 10 minutes until rabbit is done. Add a little water if sauce gets too thick. Return the green peppers and onions to mixture and add the water chestnuts. Stir thoroughly. Garnish with chopped chives. Serve over rice or noodles.

Diener Hasenpfeffer

Makes 6 servings

5	pounds cut up rabbit with giblets	4	tablespoons flour
	salt	¾	cup sour cream
4	tablespoons bacon fat or butter		freshly ground black pepper
			salt to taste

Marinate rabbit in Diener Rabbit Marinade (see below). Remove meat from marinade and pat dry. Sprinkle with salt. Heat bacon fat or butter in a casserole and when hot and bubbling, add rabbit pieces and giblets. Brown thoroughly on all sides and sprinkle with flour. Stir over moderate heat until flour begins to brown and is absorbed by the fat. If there is excess fat, pour it off. Strain marinade and gradually add it to the rabbit pieces in casserole, stirring to blend well. Cover and simmer 35 to 45 minutes, or until meat is very tender. Add salt and freshly ground pepper to taste. Just before serving, stir in sour cream and heat, but do not boil, so that the sour cream does not separate. Serve over, or with, spaetzle (page 90).

Diener Rabbit Marinade

Makes 6 servings

½	cup vinegar	4	whole cloves
1	cup dry red wine	½	tablespoon pickling spice
½	cup water	10	whole peppercorns, crushed
1	large onion, sliced	4	whole juniper berries, crushed
1	bay leaf		

Combine marinade ingredients in medium pot and simmer 15 minutes. Pour over the rabbit in a deep bowl . Marinate in refrigerator 1 to 2 days, turning meat once or twice each day.

Shish Kabunny

Makes 8 servings

2	pounds rabbit meat, cubed	2	red peppers, cut into squares
8	skewers 12-inch		for skewering
3	medium onions, cut into	18	medium button
	quarters for skewering		mushrooms, stems removed
2	medium zucchini, sliced ¼-		salt and pepper
	inch thick		

Make Shish Kabunny Marinade. Rub rabbit cubes with salt and pepper. Put cubes into bowl, add marinade. Refrigerate overnight or at least 12 hours. Stir occasionally. Drain rabbit and reserve the marinade. Pat the cubes dry on paper towels. In a hot skillet with enough oil to brown the meat cubes, turn frequently until they are evenly browned on all sides. Thread 8 skewers, alternating meat with onion, zucchini, red pepper and mushrooms. Grill over hot coals or on preheated gas grill. Baste with marinade, turning often, until the rabbit is done and the vegetables have softened, approximately 10 to 12 minutes.

Shish Kabunny Marinade

Makes 8 servings

¼	cup vegetable oil	1	teaspoon Italian seasoning,
½	cup onion, chopped		dried
¼	cup cilantro, chopped	1	clove garlic, minced
¼	cup lemon juice		

Combine all ingredients and pour over rabbit.

Spaetzle

Makes 6 servings

2¼	cups flour	¼	teaspoon nutmeg
1	teaspoon salt	2	whole eggs
¼	teaspoon baking powder	1	cup milk

Fill a 4 to 6 quart pot with water. Add a little salt and bring to a boil.

Sift together the flour, salt, baking powder and nutmeg. Add eggs and mix. Add milk gradually, beating vigorously to trap air until the batter is stiff, but smooth. Press dough flat on a plate or floured board. With a sharp knife, scrape small pieces of dough off and drop into rapidly boiling water. There should only be one layer of spaetzle at a time in the cooking water. Boil gently 3 to 5 minutes. They will float to the top. Taste one or two to make sure they are cooked. Repeat with remaining dough. Serve with Diener Hasenpfeffer (page 88).

Exotic

Alligator Étouffée

Makes 6 servings

1 pound alligator meat, julienned
2 sticks unsalted butter
½ cup green onions, chopped
4 celery stalks, chopped
1 cup bell pepper (green, red, yellow), chopped
2 garlic cloves, minced
2 cups tomatoes, diced
2 teaspoons salt
1 teaspoon pepper
2 teaspoons cayenne pepper
1 tablespoon flour
1 cup chicken or vegetable stock
¼ cup parsley, chopped

If frozen, defrost alligator meat.

Melt the butter in a large skillet over medium heat. Add the onions, celery, peppers, and garlic and cook until soft and golden. Add tomatoes and simmer for 20 minutes. Add the alligator, salt, pepper, cayenne and bring to a simmer. Dissolve flour into stock, stirring well to remove any lumps, Pour over alligator and vegetable mixture and simmer, covered, over low heat for about an hour or until tender. If gravy is too thick, add a little hot water. Sprinkle with chopped parsley and serve over rice.

Blackened Alligator Steaks

Makes 4 servings

4   alligator tail steaks, about   1 ½   teaspoons cayenne pepper
    ¾-inch thick   2   tablespoons oil for browning
1   tablespoon ground black
    pepper

Season alligator meat with black and cayenne peppers. Make Marinade for Alligator Steaks. Place meat in bowl, pour in marinade and add additional milk if needed to cover. Let marinate, refrigerated, 4 to 8 hours.

To Cook:
Preheat oven to 400°. Remove meat from marinade and discard marinade. Pat the meat dry and dredge on both sides in Blackening Seasoning (page 94). Place 2 tablespoons oil in iron skillet and heat over medium high heat until smoking. Place meat in skillet and blacken; turn and blacken other side. Place skillet of meat in oven for 10 minutes, or until tender. Serve immediately. Good with red beans and rice.

Marinade for Alligator Steaks

Makes 2 cups

2   cups milk   1   tablespoon fresh rosemary
2   teaspoons red pepper flakes   leaves

Combine all ingredients. Pour over alligator steaks and refrigerate.

Blackening Seasoning for Alligator Steaks

Makes 2 ¾ cups

3	tablespoons dried thyme	5	tablespoons ground black pepper
3	tablespoons dried oregano		
6	tablespoons garlic powder	2	tablespoons red pepper flakes, minced
4	tablespoons cayenne pepper		

Combine all ingredients in a mixing bowl. Blend well. Can be stored up to 3 months in an air-tight container in pantry.

Jamaican Curry Goat

Makes 6 servings

3	tablespoons West Indian Masala (page 95)	2	onions, sliced
½	teaspoon salt	2	tomatoes, seeded and chopped
½	teaspoon ground cardamom	½	cup green onions, sliced
½	teaspoon curry powder	4	fresh jalapeño peppers, seeded and chopped
½	teaspoon freshly ground black pepper	2	tablespoons butter
2	pounds goat meat, cubed	¼	cup vegetable oil
2	cloves garlic, minced	3	cups water

In a large bowl, combine West Indian Masala, salt, cardamom, curry powder and black pepper. Add the goat and rub the dry spices into it. Add garlic, onions, tomatoes, green onions and jalapeños. Mix well, Allow meat to marinate, covered in the refrigerator for at least 8 hours.

Remove meat from marinade and reserve marinade. Sauté meat in butter and oil in a large skillet until brown. Add water to cover and simmer until meat is very tender, about 1 hour, adding more water if necessary. Return the marinade to the meat mixture, cover and simmer 15 minutes more.

Most grocery stores carry West Indian Masala in the spice section, or you can make your own (page 95).

West Indian Masala

Makes ⅔ cup

6	tablespoons coriander seeds	1 ½	teaspoons cumin seeds
1	teaspoon fenugreek seeds	2	teaspoons ground turmeric
2	tablespoons fennel seeds	1	teaspoon ground Jamaican
1	teaspoon mustard seeds		allspice

Preheat oven to 350°. Spread all seeds on a sheet pan or cookie sheet. Roast until seeds start to pop. Shake pan and cover with additional sheet pan. Continue to roast 8 to 10 minutes more, shake pan occasionally. Be careful not to let seeds burn! Cool slightly, then grind all the seeds in a blender or spice mill. Add turmeric and Jamaican allspice, blend well. Unused masala can be stored in a tightly covered jar.

Asian Stir-Fried Kangaroo

Makes 6 servings

1	tablespoon peanut oil	2	tablespoons sweet chili sauce
1	large onion, chopped fine	2	tablespoons soy sauce
1	teaspoon garlic, minced	2	cups beef or game stock
1	teaspoon fresh minced ginger	½	cup bean sprouts
1	pound kangaroo filet, cubed	1	cup Chinese chow mein
1	small bunch bok choy,		noodles
	chopped		salt and pepper
⅓	cup chopped cilantro plus		
	sprigs for garnish		

Heat wok over high heat until nearly smoking. Add oil and tip wok to spread evenly. When very hot, stir-fry onion, garlic, and ginger 1 to 2 minutes, then stir in the kangaroo. Sauté until kangaroo is browned. Add bok choy, cilantro, sweet chili sauce and soy sauce. Stir well, then pour in stock and add bean sprouts. Simmer 10 minutes. Season with salt and pepper and garnish with sprigs of cilantro and chow mein noodles.

Rattlesnake Ravioli with Jicama & Roasted Red Pepper Sauce

Makes 4 servings

4   tablespoons unsalted butter
1   stalk celery trimmed and finely, chopped
1   carrot peeled and finely, chopped
1   small onion, finely chopped
10 ounces boneless rattlesnake meat, cut into 1-inch pieces
¼   cup dry Marsala wine
2   egg yolks

⅓   cup pepper jack cheese, finely grated
⅓   cup Parmesan cheese, finely grated
    salt and freshly ground pepper to taste
12 ounces freshly made pasta dough
1   tablespoon all-purpose flour
    Salt and pepper to taste

Snake filling:

In a frying pan, melt butter over low heat. Add the celery, carrot and onion. Sauté, stirring frequently, until the onion is translucent, about 5 minutes. Add the snake, raise the heat slightly and sauté, stirring until the snake is golden, about 10 minutes. Pour in the Marsala, lower the heat, cover and cook for 5 minutes. Remove the pan from the heat, drain any liquid still remaining and reserve. Turn out the contents onto a cutting board or place in a food processor and chop very finely. Place in a bowl; add the egg yolks, all of the pepper jack cheese and half of the Parmesan cheese and some of the reserved liquid if too dry.

Mix thoroughly and season to taste with salt and pepper. Set aside. Prepare the Egg Pasta Dough (page 100) and cut into strips 2⅜ inches wide by 12 inches long. On half of the strips, place small mounds of the snake mixture at 2⅜-inch intervals. Brush the edges of the strips and wet in between the mounds with cold water. Cover the filled strips with the remaining pasta strips. To seal, press along the edges and around the

(Continued on next page)

Rattlesnake Ravioli *(continued from previous page)*

stuffing. Using a pastry wheel with fluted edge, cut the strips into 2-inch squares. Lightly dust a work surface with flour or fine cornmeal and, with a spatula, arrange the ravioli on it. Bring 5 quarts of salted water to boil in a large pot. Add the ravioli to the boiling water and cook until they rise to the surface, about 2 to 3 minutes. Remove ravioli with a slotted spoon. Drain well, and arrange on a warm platter or in a bowl. Pour Jicama and Roasted Red Pepper Sauce over ravioli and sprinkle with the remaining Parmesan cheese.

Jicama and Roasted Red Pepper Sauce

Makes 2 cups

1	cup peeled jicama in ¼-inch dice	1	poblano chili, seeded and diced
4	red peppers, roasted* and diced	1	cup beef stock
1	teaspoon shallots, chopped	3	tablespoons cold heavy cream
1	teaspoon garlic, minced	¼	cup sour cream
			salt and pepper to taste

Place jicama, roasted red peppers, shallots, garlic, chili and beef stock in a sauté pan. Bring to a boil and simmer until almost all liquid is evaporated. Place mixture into food processor or blender and puree. Remove and place in saucepan on low heat or in double boiler. Add heavy cream, sour cream, salt and pepper to taste and blend.

* To roast peppers place directly over open gas flame, turning frequently until blackened. Or place peppers on a pan and broil in oven until blackened. Place blackened peppers in a paper bag for 10-15 minutes. Peel off blackened skin, remove seeds and stem, and cut roasted peppers into dice.

Rattlesnake Steaks

Makes 4 servings

4   snake filet steaks 1 inch to
    1 ½ inches thick, boneless
5   tablespoons butter
1   pound button mushrooms,
    sliced
2   tablespoons onion, minced

½   cup Cabernet Sauvignon or
    other red wine
1   tablespoon garlic, minced
1   tablespoon flour
    salt and pepper to taste
½   cup fresh cilantro, chopped

Preheat oven to 250°.

Heat 2 tablespoons butter in skillet, sauté snake filets 5 minutes on each side. Remove filets and keep warm in oven, wrapped in foil. Add 2 more tablespoons of butter to skillet, melt and sauté mushrooms, onions and garlic, until tender. Add red wine, simmer until reduced by half.

Mix 1 tablespoon butter and flour to form a paste, when sauce is reduced by half, add butter paste, stirring constantly for 2 minutes, or until thickened. Add salt and pepper to taste. Remove snake steaks from oven, serve on platter or individual plates, pouring sauce over snake and garnishing with fresh cilantro. A nice accompaniment is fresh green beans and fettuccine (page 100).

Egg Pasta Dough

Makes 6 servings

2⅓ cups all-purpose flour, plus   3   extra large eggs
½ cup for board and extra
for sprinkling

Hand Method: Heap the 2⅓ cups of flour on a clean, floured surface, making a well in the center. Break the eggs into the well, and using a fork or your fingers, combine the eggs with the flour in a circular motion, until all of the eggs are combined with the flour. Continue to knead until smooth. Place a damp towel over the pasta dough and let rest for 20 minutes. Pull off a piece of dough the size of an egg. Roll out until very thin. Cut into fettuccine by hand or use a pasta wheel. Let dry slightly before boiling.

Food Processor Method: Place the flour into the container of a food processor. With the motor running, add the eggs one at a time. When the dough forms a ball on the blade, remove it, cover and let rest for 30 minutes. Roll out using a hand-crank pasta rolling machine. Cut into pasta shapes. Dry slightly, then boil.

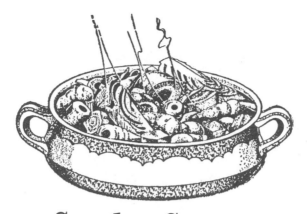

Stocks, Soups,
Gumbo, Chilies & Stews

Game Stock

Makes 3 quarts

1	onion, cut in eighths	3	sprigs fresh sage
2	carrots, cut in 3-inch or 5-inch lengths	3	sprigs fresh thyme
		1	celery stalk
5	pounds venison bones (or other game bones)	5	peppercorns
		5	juniper berries
6	sprigs fresh parsley		water

Preheat oven to 400°. Spread the onion, carrots and game bones in a roasting pan or baking sheet and roast for 15 minutes, shaking the pan every few minutes,until the bones are browned. Transfer browned bones and vegetables to a large pot. Add 1 cup of water to baking pan or sheet and scrape with a spatula over medium heat, to release the caramelized cooking particles. Add this liquid to the pot along with the parsley, sage and thyme tied together with string or a twist tie, the celery, peppercorns and juniper berries. Add 5 quarts of cold water and turn the heat on high. Just before the stock boils, reduce heat to simmer and cook for 4 to 5 hours, stirring occasionally. Skim off fat or scum that may rise to the top. Set aside to cool. Strain and discard solids. The stock may be stored covered in refrigerator for 5 days or frozen up to 3 months.

Wild Duck Stock

Makes 2 quarts

2	wild ducks, cleaned and dressed	2	small carrots, peeled and diced
2	celery stalks, diced	1	tablespoon salt
1	small onion, diced	1	gallon water

In a large pot, combine ducks, diced celery stalks, diced onion and carrots, salt and water. Bring to boil and simmer, partially covered, for 3 hours. Skim excess foam, as needed. Remove all solids and strain. Stock may be stored covered in refrigerator for 5 days or frozen up to 3 months. Use in gumbo or anywhere you would use a poultry stock.

White Game Chili

Makes 8–10 servings

1	pound white Great Northern beans
3	quarts light game or chicken stock
3	cups chopped celery
2	large onions, diced
1	jalapeño pepper minced, seeds removed
2	green bell peppers, diced
2	leeks, sliced, white part only
5	cloves garlic, minced
2	tablespoons cumin
1	tablespoon dried oregano
1	tablespoon ground white pepper
³/₄	cup flour
2	quarts half-and-half (fat free OK)
2	pounds diced, cooked pheasant, rabbit, or dove
	salt to taste

Garnish: grated Cheddar or Monterey Jack cheese, sliced scallions, crumbled bacon

In a large stockpot, soak beans overnight in water to cover—or use the quick soak method: Cover beans with water, bring to a boil, then set off the heat and leave covered for an hour. Drain beans and add the chicken stock to beans. Bring to a boil, covered then reduce to simmer and cook for about 40 minutes, or until the beans are softened, but not mushy. Uncover and add the celery, onions, peppers, leeks, garlic, and spices. Continue to simmer for about an hour. Combine the flour with a little of the half and half. Using a whisk, carefully add the flour to the bean mixture, blending well. Then, add the rest of the half and half and game meat, stirring to blend well. Continue to simmer for about 30 minutes. Add salt to taste. Serve in warmed bowls topped with grated Cheddar or Monterey Jack, sliced scallions and crumbled bacon.

Crockpot Venison Chili

Makes 4 – 6 servings

4   slices bacon

1½   pounds venison steak, cut into cubes

1   large green bell pepper, diced

1   large red bell pepper, diced

1   jalapeño pepper, remove seeds if you don't like it hot

1   28-ounce can of crushed tomatoes, or whole tomatoes chopped

1   tablespoon cumin powder

1   teaspoon or more of chili powder

½   can of beer

Garnish: sour cream, shredded Cheddar and diced Vidalia onions

Cook the bacon until crisp. Drain, crumble and reserve. Leave three tablespoons of the bacon fat in the pan. Lightly brown the venison in bacon fat. Scrape venison into slow cooker. Add remaining ingredients to slow cooker (except for the garnishes). Stir well, cover and cook on low for about 8 hours, or until venison is tender. Serve in warmed bowls topped with sour cream, shredded cheddar and raw onions.

Tantalizing Turtle Soup

Makes 10 servings

1½ pounds turtle meat (substitute venison or veal — for a mock soup)
2 teaspoons salt
½ to 1 teaspoon cayenne pepper, or to taste
6 cups water
1 stick butter
½ cup flour
1½ cups onions, chopped
½ cup bell peppers, chopped
¼ cup celery, chopped
3 bay leaves
1 teaspoon dried thyme
2 tablespoons garlic, chopped
1 cup canned tomatoes, diced
1 tablespoon Worcestershire sauce
1 lemon, juice and zest
½ cup dry sherry
¼ cup parsley, chopped
½ cup green onions, chopped
5 hard boiled eggs, finely chopped
lemon or lime slices for garnish

Put the turtle meat in a large saucepan with 1 teaspoon salt, ¼ teaspoon cayenne, and water. Bring to a boil. Skim off any foam that rises to the surface. Reduce the heat to medium and simmer uncovered for 30 minutes. Transfer the meat to a platter, let cool and cut into cubes. Set aside and reserve the stock.

In a large saucepan, combine the butter and flour over medium high heat. Stir constantly to make a dark brown roux, about 10 minutes. Add the onions, peppers and celery. Stir for 2 to 3 minutes until the vegetables are slightly soft. Add the bay leaves, thyme and garlic and cook for additional few minutes. Add the tomatoes and return turtle meat to pot. Cook stirring occasionally for 6 to 8 minutes. Add the Worcestershire sauce, the remaining salt and cayenne, the reserved turtle stock, lemon juice and zest and sherry. Bring to a boil. Reduce the heat to medium and simmer for 10 to 15 minutes. Add the parsley, green onions and eggs. Simmer uncovered for about 45 minutes to an hour or until turtle or substitute meat is tender. Serve in bowls and garnish with lemon or lime slices.

Tennessee Wild Duck Gumbo

Makes 12 servings

2	wild ducks, cleaned and dressed	¼	teaspoon red pepper
2	celery stalks	½	tablespoon black pepper
1	small onion, diced	2	cups celery, chopped
2	small carrots, diced	2	cups onion, chopped
1	tablespoon salt	1	pound smoked Andouille sausage
1	gallon water	1	pound okra
1	cup flour	1	16-ounce can diced tomatoes
¾	cup vegetable oil	½	cup scallions, sliced
1	cup bell peppers, chopped		filé powder, optional

Step One: To make the stock—
In large pot combine the ducks, celery, onion, diced carrots, salt, and water. Bring to a boil and simmer for 3 hours, skimming off the foam from time to time.

Step Two: To make the gumbo—
Make the roux. Combine flour and vegetable oil and cook, stirring, over medium low until dark brown, 20 to 30 minutes. Be careful not to let the roux scorch. Add the bell peppers, red and black pepper, celery, and onion. Sauté until vegetables are softened and reserve. Remove the ducks from the stock and reduce the broth 2 to 2½ quarts. Strain and pour broth over the roux, stirring to blend, with whisk. Simmer the gumbo for 20 minutes or more. Thin with water or chicken stock, if too thick.

Remove all the meat from the bones and skin, cut in small pieces, and add to the gumbo. Broil the sausage (turning to brown evenly), slice, and add to the gumbo. Add the okra and tomatoes and continue to cook until the okra is soft and the gumbo is thick. Add the scallions during the last 5 minutes and bring to a boil.

Serve over white rice with Tabasco® sauce as needed. If desired, sprinkle with filé powder.

Larose Duck Camp Gumbo

Makes 10 servings

3	large wild ducks, cut up, skin on	2	cups red wine
2	teaspoons oil, for browning	1	gallon duck/chicken stock
2	large onions, chopped	1	cup canned diced tomatoes
1	cup celery, chopped	1	pound smoked Italian sausage links, cut into thin slices or half moons
½	cup butter or oil		
¾	cup flour	4	medium turnips, diced
2	tablespoons mixed Italian seasoning Cajun/blackening season to taste	2	medium parsnips, diced
		1	cup green onions, sliced for garnish
1	tablespoon garlic	2	tablespoons gumbo filé, for garnish

Brown ducks in 2 teaspoons of oil in stock pot at high heat. Remove ducks, add onions and celery and sauté until lightly brown. Add the butter or oil and cook over medium heat, until melted and starting to brown. Add flour and reduce heat to low; cook, stirring frequently until roux is a light brown color and has a nutty aroma, about 15 minutes. Add herbs, Cajun seasoning and garlic and turn up heat to high. After 2 minutes, add red wine and stir in until well blended. Add ducks, and when they have simmered at least 10 minutes, add all remaining ingredients, except the turnips, parsnips, and garnishes. After ducks have simmered approximately 1½ hours, add turnips and parsnips. When ducks start to pull off the bones and are tender, remove bones and skin. Cut in small pieces and return to pot.

If serving as is, add the green onions and filé powder. If serving over rice, top with green onions and filé powder.

Brunswick Stew

Makes 6 to 8 servings

5	pounds squirrel, disjointed	1	quart tomatoes, drained
6	pieces bacon, diced, fried and fat reserved	½	teaspoon cayenne pepper
		4	teaspoons thyme
3	onions, sliced	2	cups fresh/frozen lima beans
	salt and pepper to taste	2	cups fresh/frozen corn
2	quarts beef or game stock to cover	2	cups fresh/frozen okra
			fine bread crumbs
4	potatoes, peeled and diced		

Brown the meat and onion in hot bacon fat in a 6 to 8 quart Dutch oven. Season with salt and pepper. Add stock to cover meat and simmer until tender. Remove the bones, fat, skin from the meat. Add the potatoes, tomatoes, diced bacon, cayenne and thyme. Cook slowly for 45 minutes, then add the fresh lima beans, corn and okra. Cook until vegetables are tender. Thicken with fine bread crumbs and adjust seasonings to taste before serving in heated bowls.

Galliano Game Jambalaya

Makes 8 to 10 servings

4	pounds assorted wild game cut into pieces or game birds	3	cups chicken or game stock
3	tablespoons bacon drippings or oil	1	cup red wine
		1	tablespoon Worcestershire sauce
2	large onions, chopped	2	bunches green onions, chopped
2	cups celery, chopped		
4	cups mixed bell peppers (red, green, yellow), chopped	½	cup parsley, chopped
		2	tablespoons creole / blackening seasoning
2	cups diced stewed tomatoes		
1	pound cooked Andouille or smoked sausage, sliced thick	2	tablespoons Italian herb seasoning
2	tablespoons garlic, minced	4	tablespoons Galliano Italian liqueur
4	cups rice		

Preheat oven to 350°.

In a 6 to 8 quart dutch oven, heat bacon drippings or oil and sauté wild game in batches until browned on all sides. Remove. Add onions, celery and peppers and continue cooking until soft and lightly browned. Add tomatoes, sausage and garlic and continue to cook for a few minutes. Add rice and stir, cooking for 2 to 3 minutes. Add remaining ingredients except the Galliano liqueur. Stir well and bring to a simmer. Replace wild game in pot, stir well and cover. Place in oven for 45 minutes to an hour or until game and rice are tender. Top with Galliano Liqueur and stir gently. Greek Ouzo can be substituted for the Galliano.

Wild Game Chili

Makes 6 to 8 servings

2	tablespoons vegetable oil	3	tablespoons chili powder
3	cloves garlic, chopped	10	tomatoes, peeled and chopped
2	onions, chopped		
1	green bell pepper, chopped	1	cup red kidney beans, cooked
3	pounds wild game* meat, chopped		
		2	jalapeño peppers (optional)
1	teaspoon ground cumin	1	can of beer OR
1	teaspoon ground oregano	½	cup Jack Daniels

Heat oil in a large heavy skillet or pot. Add garlic, onions and green pepper. Sauté until soft, about 5 to 7 minutes. Add chopped wild game meat and lightly brown on all surfaces. If necessary, drain off some of the fat that has accumulated. Add remaining ingredients and simmer for 1 hour or slightly longer. Add cover during cooking time, and slightly tilt it so steam can escape. Check often and stir to prevent sticking. Skim off fat as it rises. Best if allowed to sit, tightly covered, for an hour after cooking is complete.

* You can use cougar, venison, duck or other wild game.

Serving Ideas: Serve with cornbread or Texas Toast.

Wild Turkey & Game Sausage Gumbo

Makes 12 servings

¹/₂	cup oil	1	small wild turkey, cleaned and quartered
¹/₂	cup flour - for roux		
1	large onion, chopped	1	quart game stock
1	cup diced celery	1	tablespoon Creole/Cajun seasoning
1	large green pepper, chopped		
1	bunch green onions, chopped	2	teaspoons poultry seasoning Sprigs of fresh thyme
4	cloves garlic, minced	1	pound duck or game sausage, in 1-inch chunks
	Parsley for garnish		

Heat the oil over medium heat. Add the flour and stir well. Cook, stirring constantly until roux turns a rich brown, taking care not to burn it. Add the onions, celery, bell pepper and green onions and cook until softened. Add the garlic and cook a minute. Add the turkey, stock and seasonings, except parsley. Bring to a boil, then reduce heat and simmer one hour. Add the sausage and continue to cook another 45 minutes, or until turkey is falling off the bones. Cool and remove turkey skin and bones. Chill gumbo, if time permits, and remove any excess fat that rises to the top. Reheat gumbo and serve, topped with chopped parsley. If desired, place a bit of cooked rice in the bowl before adding gumbo.

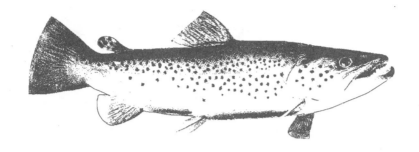

Trout

Smoked Trout Soufflé in a Phyllo Crust

Makes 8 servings

8 17x12-inch phyllo sheets, thawed	2 home-smoked trout fillets (about 1/2 pound total) or purchased smoked trout
5 1/2 tablespoons unsalted butter	
1 1/2 tablespoons all-purpose flour	6 large eggs
1/2 cup whole milk	1 1/2 teaspoons drained bottled horseradish
1/2 cup heavy cream	2 tablespoons fresh dill leaves

Cover phyllo stack with overlapping sheets of plastic wrap and then a damp kitchen towel.

Melt 4 tablespoons of the butter. Arrange 1 phyllo sheet on a work surface and brush with some melted butter. Arrange another sheet to overlap the first and form a 17-inch square and brush with butter. Continue layering with remaining 6 sheets and butter. Drape phyllo stack over a 10-inch tart pan with a removable bottom and fit phyllo into pan. Crumple overhang against inside edge of rim to create a ragged edge that stands about 1 inch above rim. Chill shell, loosely covered, until firm, at least 3 hours.

Preheat oven to 375°F.

Prick bottom of shell all over with a fork and bake in middle of oven until golden, about 15 minutes. Cool shell in pan on a rack. Shell may be made 1 day ahead and kept, covered at cool room temperature.

In a saucepan melt remaining 1½ tablespoons butter over moderately low heat and whisk in flour. Cook roux, stirring, 3 minutes and whisk in milk and heavy cream. Bring mixture to a boil, whisking constantly. Simmer, whisking occasionally for 3 minutes. Season mixture with salt and pepper and cool.

(Continued on next page)

Smoked Trout Soufflé in a Phyllo Crust (continued)

Discard skin from trout and break fish into small pieces. Separate eggs. In a food processor pulse together milk mixture, trout, horseradish, and dill until smooth and transfer to a large bowl.

In another large bowl with an electric mixer, beat whites with a pinch of salt until they just hold stiff peaks. Stir one-fourth of the whites into trout mixture to lighten and fold in remaining whites gently but thoroughly.

Pour soufflé mixture into shell and run tip of knife around edge of soufflé to aid rising. Bake soufflé on a baking sheet in lower third of oven until puffed and golden brown, about 25 minutes. Serve soufflé immediately.

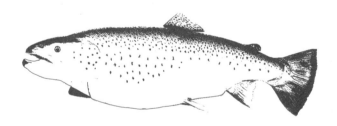

Scrambled Eggs with Smoked Trout and Green Onions

Makes 4 servings

Toasted onion bagels are great with this.

8   large eggs
1   home-smoked trout filet or
    one 4 1/2-ounce package
    smoked trout fillets, broken
    into half-inch pieces
4   ounces cream cheese, cut
    into half-inch pieces, room
    temperature
1/2 cup chopped green onions

1 1/2 tablespoons chopped fresh
    dill or 1/2 teaspoon dried
    dill
1/4 teaspoon cayenne
1   tablespoon lemon juice
    salt and pepper
2 1/2 tablespoons butter

Garnish: Fresh dill sprigs,
    optional

Whisk eggs in large bowl to blend. Add trout, cream cheese, green onions, chopped dill, cayenne and lemon juice. Season lightly with salt and generously with pepper; stir to mix.

Melt butter in large nonstick skillet over medium heat. Add egg mixture and stir slowly until eggs just hold together and are cooked through but still moist, about 4 minutes. Divide egg mixture among 4 plates. Garnish with dill sprigs, if desired, and serve.

Smoked Trout and Roasted Pepper Bruschetta

Makes 14 Toasts

Can be prepared in 45 minutes or less.

3/4 teaspoon caraway seeds, crushed
1 1/2 tablespoons fresh lemon juice
1 teaspoon Dijon mustard
1 teaspoon minced shallots
1 smoked trout (about 1/2 pound), head, tail, skin, and bones discarded
1 7-ounce jar roasted red peppers, drained and chopped

2 tablespoons chopped fresh parsley leaves
Salt and pepper to taste
14 French bread slices, cut 1/4-inch thick (about 2 ounces of 1 baguette), toasted and rubbed with cut edge of 1/2 garlic clove

In a bowl stir together caraway seeds, lemon juice, mustard, and shallots and add trout, mashing with a fork until finely flaked. Gently stir in roasted peppers and parsley and season with salt and pepper. Top toasts with trout mixture.

Serves two generously as a light main course, or may be used as hors d'oeuvres for four.

Pan-Fried Trout with Bacon

Makes 4-6 servings

Steamed spinach and parsleyed baby red potatoes round out this seasonal plate.

8	bacon slices	1/4	cup fresh lemon juice
10	tablespoons butter	4	teaspoons drained capers
4	trout, 8-10 ounces each, filleted	4	teaspoons chopped fresh tarragon
	All purpose flour		Salt and pepper
2	cups thinly sliced green onions		

Cook bacon in large skillet over medium heat until crisp about 8-10 minutes. Transfer to paper towels to drain. Crumble bacon and reserve. Reserve bacon drippings. Add back 3 tablespoons of drippings to skillet. Add 1 tablespoon butter and stir to melt. Sprinkle fish with salt and pepper.

Coat flesh side of half the fish filets with flour; shake off excess. Add coated fish, flesh side down, to skillet. Cook 2 minutes. Turn fish over. Cook until just opaque in center, about 2 minutes. Transfer fish to warm platter and reserve. Repeat coating and cooking of rest of fish. Pour off drippings from skillet; wipe skillet clean. Melt 8 tablespoons butter in same skillet over medium heat. Add all but 1/4 cup onions; sauté 4 minutes. Stir in bacon, lemon juice, capers, and tarragon. Season sauce with salt and pepper. Arrange cooked fish on platter. Pour some sauce over fish. Sprinkle fish with green onions. Pass remaining sauce at the table.

Pumpkin-Seed-Crusted Trout

Makes 4 servings

This recipe can be prepared in 45 minutes or less.

1	cup loosely packed fresh cilantro sprigs	Salt and pepper
3/4	cup hulled green pumpkin seeds* (about 1/4 pound)	2 tablespoons olive oil
2	large eggs	2 tablespoons fresh lime juice
1/2	cup all-purpose flour	1/2 cup dry white wine
4	small trout fillets with skin, 3 to 4 ounces each	3/4 stick (6 tablespoons) cold unsalted butter

* Available at natural foods stores.

Finely chop cilantro and reserve. In a sealable plastic bag, lightly crush pumpkin seeds with a rolling pin. Lightly beat eggs in a shallow dish. Have flour and pumpkin seeds ready in 2 separate shallow dishes. With tweezers remove any fine bones from fillets and season trout with salt and pepper. Dredge flesh side of 1 fillet in flour, shaking off excess, and dip flesh side in eggs, letting excess drip off. Coat egg-dipped side of fillet with pumpkin seeds and transfer, seed side up, to a plate. Coat remaining fillets in same manner.

In a 12-inch nonstick skillet heat olive oil over moderate heat until hot but not smoking and cook fillets, seed sides down, until golden, about 3 minutes. Turn fillets carefully with a spatula and cook skin side down over low heat until just cooked through, about 3 minutes more. Transfer fillets with a spatula to a heated platter and keep warm while making sauce.

In a small heavy saucepan boil lime juice and wine until reduced by half, about 2 minutes. Reduce heat to low. Cut butter into pieces and add 1 piece at a time, whisking until incorporated and sauce is smooth. Remove pan from heat. Add cilantro and season to taste with salt.

Spoon sauce over trout fillets.

Cornmeal-Crusted Trout with Hazelnut Butter

Makes 4 servings

1	cup cornmeal	1	tablespoon vegetable oil
1	cup all-purpose flour	3/4	cup hazelnuts, chopped
	Salt and pepper	1/3	cup fresh lemon juice
4	boned trout, heads	1/2	cup chopped fresh parsley
	discarded, halved lengthwise		Lemon wedges, for garnish
8	tablespoons butter		

Combine cornmeal and flour in pie pan. Season with salt and pepper. Coat trout with flour mixture. Melt 1 tablespoon butter with 1/2 tablespoon oil in heavy large skillet over medium-high heat. Add 4 trout pieces; cook until just cooked through, about 2 minutes per side. Transfer to platter. Melt 1 tablespoon butter with 1/2 tablespoon oil in same skillet. Add remaining trout; cook until just cooked through. Transfer to platter. Keep warm.

Wipe out any burned bits from skillet. Melt remaining 6 tablespoons butter in same skillet over medium-low heat. Add hazelnuts and sauté until brown. Add lemon juice and boil until slightly thickened, scraping up any browned bits, about 1 minute. Add parsley. Season with salt and pepper and pour over fish. Garnish with lemon.

Cold Poached Salmon Trout

Makes 6 servings

This fish is chilled overnight, so begin the recipe a day ahead. Serve with a Riesling.

3 cups dry white wine
1 1/2 cups water
1 onion, cut into 1/2-inch-thick rounds
2 teaspoons black peppercorns
2 teaspoons salt

8 salmon trout steaks or salmon steaks, 5 to 6 ounces each, cut 3/4 to 1-inch thick

1 12-ounce jar sweet gherkin pickles, coarsely chopped
1/2 cup chopped fresh parsley

Divide first 5 ingredients between 2 heavy large skillets. Arrange 4 fish steaks in each skillet. Bring liquid just to simmer over medium-low heat. Gently simmer until fish is opaque in center, about 6 minutes. Remove from heat. Using metal spatula, carefully turn fish over in skillet. Cool fish 1 hour in poaching liquid. Transfer fish and liquid to large glass baking dish. Cover and chill at least 1 day or up to 2 days.

Mix pickles and parsley in bowl. Serve fish with pickle mixture. Great as an appetizer or fish course, or served over salad greens as a light lunch.

Trout with Pecan and Pine Nut Crust

Makes 4 servings

1/4 cup pine nuts (about 1 1/2 ounces)

1/4 cup pecans (about 1 1/4 ounces)

1 tablespoon plus 1 teaspoon sesame seeds

4 whole boned trout

1 tablespoon plus 1 teaspoon butter

1 large garlic clove, minced
Salt and pepper

2 tablespoons vegetable oil

Parsley or dill sprigs, for garnish

Finely chop pine nuts and pecans in food processor, using on/off turns, being careful not to purée. Transfer to shallow bowl. Mix in sesame seeds. Open trout and place skin side down on large baking sheet.

Stir butter and garlic in small saucepan over low heat until butter melts. Brush garlic butter over trout. Sprinkle nut mixture over trout; press to adhere. Season with salt and pepper. Chill uncovered for 30 minutes.

Preheat oven to 400°F. Heat 1 tablespoon oil in large nonstick skillet over medium-high heat. Place 2 trout, nut side down, into skillet. Cook 2 minutes. Using spatula turn trout, nut side up, onto baking sheet. Repeat with remaining oil and trout. Bake trout until opaque in center, about 5 minutes. Serve on warmed plates garnished with fresh parsley or dill sprigs.

Pan-Fried Trout with Green Onions

Makes 2 servings

If you don't have whole, boned trout, you can use four fillets. Steamed baby potatoes and sautéed carrot and zucchini matchsticks are appropriate side dishes.

2	whole trout, 11 to 12 ounces, boned	3	green onions, chopped
	All purpose flour	1/2	cup dry white wine
1	tablespoon olive oil	1	tablespoon butter

Open each trout flat like a book. Sprinkle generously with salt and pepper. Dust trout with flour and shake off excess. Heat 1/2 tablespoon olive oil in heavy, large skillet over medium-high heat. Add 1 trout and sauté until coating is crisp and trout is just opaque in center about 2 minutes per side. Transfer trout to plate and tent with foil to keep warm. Repeat with remaining 1/2 tablespoon oil and remaining trout.

Wipe out skillet with paper towels. Set aside 2 tablespoons green onions. Add remaining green onions, wine and butter to same skillet. Simmer over medium heat until mixture is almost reduced to glaze, stirring occasionally, about 3 minutes. Spoon sauce over trout. Sprinkle trout with reserved 2 tablespoons green onions and serve.

Recipe can be doubled for more servings.

Spinach Salad with Smoked Trout and Tart Apple

Makes 4 servings

1   tart apple such as Granny Smith

3   tablespoons extra-virgin olive oil

2   tablespoons fresh lemon juice

1/2   teaspoon Dijon mustard

8   cups packed spinach (about 12 ounces), washed well, dried, and coarse stems discarded

2   smoked trout (about 8 ounces each), skin and bones discarded and fish broken into bite-size pieces

1/3   cup sliced almonds, toasted golden

1/3   cup dried currants
Salt and pepper

Wash and core the apple and cut into 1-inch wedges. Cut wedges crosswise into 1/4-inch-thick slices.

In a large salad bowl whisk together oil, lemon juice, and mustard and add apple, tossing to coat. Add remaining ingredients, tossing to combine, and season with salt and pepper.

Nice as a light lunch or first course.

Trout with Cucumber and Sour Cream

Makes 4 servings

A delicate and sophisticated main course. Use trout fillets with skin or use two whole trout, cleaned.

1	large cucumber peeled and very thinly sliced into rounds	1	cup sour cream
		1	teaspoon grated lemon zest
3	teaspoons chopped fresh dill	2	tablespoons ($1/4$ stick) butter, melted
$2^{1}/_{2}$	teaspoons fresh lemon juice	2	pounds fresh trout (approximately) – filets with skin or whole, cleaned

Preheat oven to 375°F. Combine cucumber, $1^{1}/_{2}$ teaspoons dill and $1^{1}/_{2}$ teaspoons lemon juice in medium bowl. Season with salt and pepper. Toss to coat. Combine sour cream, lemon zest and remaining 1 teaspoon lemon juice in small bowl; season with salt and pepper and stir to blend.

Brush baking sheet with some of the melted butter. Arrange trout fillets, skin side down, on prepared sheet. Brush trout with remaining butter and sprinkle with salt and pepper. Bake until just opaque in center, about 10 minutes.

Divide cucumbers among 4 plates. Using spatula, place trout atop cucumbers. Spoon sour cream sauce over. Sprinkle with remaining $1^{1}/_{2}$ teaspoons dill.

Whole Baked Trout with Mushrooms

Makes 4 servings

3 tablespoons butter

3 tablespoons vegetable oil

6 cups sliced mixed fresh wild mushrooms (such as portobello, cremini and stemmed shiitake; about 12 ounces)

1 1/2 cups chopped onion

1 large celery stalk, chopped

3 tablespoons minced fresh parsley

1 1/2 teaspoons dried thyme

3 ounces thinly sliced prosciutto, chopped

4 whole trout (about 12 ounces each), cleaned, boned

2 tablespoons fresh lemon juice

1/4 cup (1/2 stick) butter, melted

parsley for garnish

Melt butter with oil in heavy large skillet over medium heat. Add mushrooms, onion, celery, parsley and thyme; cook until mushrooms brown and all liquid evaporates, stirring frequently, about 20 minutes. Remove from heat. Stir in prosciutto. Season filling to taste with salt and pepper. Cool. Filling can be prepared 1 day ahead. (Cover and refrigerate.)

Preheat oven to 350°F. Butter large baking sheet. Open fish like a book. Drizzle with lemon juice. Sprinkle with salt and pepper. Spoon filling over 1 side of each fish, dividing equally. Fold second side over, enclosing filling. Placed stuffed fish on prepared sheet. Brush outside of fish with melted butter.

Bake until cooked through, about 30 minutes. Transfer to platter. Garnish with parsley.

Smoked Trout Cakes with Horseradish Cream

Makes 4 servings

1 1/2 cups flaked smoked trout or other smoked white fish
2 tablespoons chopped green onions
2 teaspoons drained capers
1/2 teaspoon grated lemon peel
1/4 teaspoon ground pepper
   salt
1 large egg, beaten to blend
1/4 cup whipping cream
1 cup fresh breadcrumbs made from French bread

2 tablespoons vegetable oil, or more

Horseradish Cream
1 cup sour cream (light is OK)
3 tablespoons drained horseradish, or to taste
1 scallion, sliced thin
1/2 teaspoon Old Bay seasoning

Blend together the ingredients for the Horseradish Cream. Serve with the trout cakes.

Combine trout, green onions, capers, lemon peel and pepper in medium bowl. Season with salt. Stir in egg, cream and half the breadcrumbs to blend. Form mixture into eight 1/2-inch-thick fish cakes, using 1/4 cup of the mixture for each fish cake.

Place remaining breadcrumbs in shallow dish. Roll fish cakes in breadcrumbs, coating completely. Heat 2 tablespoons oil in large skillet over medium heat. Working in batches and adding more oil as necessary, cook fish cakes until golden brown, about 3 minutes per side. Serve with Horseradish Cream. Good with a mixed green salad on the side.

Pan-Fried Trout with Red Onion and Orange Relish

Makes 2 servings

This recipe can be completed in no time. Complete the menu with roasted potatoes and steamed spinach.

1	medium orange	2	tablespoons white wine vinegar
3	tablespoons chopped fresh mint		Salt and pepper
2	tablespoons olive oil	1	1 1/3-pound trout, boned, cut in half lengthwise
2/3	cup chopped red onion		Yellow cornmeal

Grate 1 teaspoon zest from orange. Cut off remaining peel and pith and discard. Cut orange into 1/2-inch pieces. Mix orange pieces, zest and mint in small bowl. Heat 1/2 tablespoon oil in a large, heavy skillet over medium heat. Add onion, then vinegar. Toss until just heated through, about 1 minute. Add onion mixture to orange mixture (do not clean skillet). Season relish with salt and pepper.

Sprinkle fish with salt and pepper. Sprinkle on all sides with cornmeal. Heat remaining 1 1/2 tablespoons oil in same skillet over medium-high heat. Add fish, sauté until crisp outside and just opaque in center, about 4 minutes per side. Transfer fish to warmed plates; top with relish.

Recipe can be doubled to serve four.

Smoked Trout, Watercress and Apple Salad with Creamy Horseradish Dressing

Makes 6 servings

An elegant salad that will add a sophisticated touch to any menu.

1 cup heavy cream	6 cups trimmed watercress
1/3 cup prepared horseradish	sprigs (about 2 large
4 tablespoons olive oil,	bunches
divided	1/2 cup very thinly sliced red
2 tablespoons plus 2 teaspoons	onion
Champagne vinegar	2 red apples, cored, thinly
2 teaspoons finely chopped	sliced
fresh dill	9 ounces smoked trout or
1/8 teaspoon cayenne pepper	smoked whitefish chubs,
Salt and pepper	coarsely flaked
	Fresh dill sprigs, for
	garnish, optional

Whisk cream, horseradish, 2 tablespoons olive oil, 2 tablespoons vinegar, chopped dill and cayenne in small bowl to blend. Season to taste with salt and pepper. Place watercress in large bowl. Add 1/3 cup cream dressing, 2 tablespoons olive oil and 2 teaspoons Champagne vinegar and toss to coat. Season to taste with salt and pepper. Mound watercress in center of each of 6 plates. Top with sliced onion. Fan apple slices atop salad. Top with smoked trout. Spoon additional dressing over each plate. Garnish with dill sprigs, if desired, and serve.

Pecan-Crusted Trout with Orange-Rosemary Butter Sauce

Makes 4 servings

Remove the head, tail and bones from the trout, then cut each trout into two fillets, leaving the skin intact.

For Trout:
2   cups pecans (about 8 ounces)
1   cup all-purpose flour
2   large (12 to 14-ounce) trout filets, skin on
    salt and pepper
3   large egg whites, beaten to blend

For sauce:
1 1/2 cups fresh orange juice
1   cup dry white wine
2/3 cup chopped shallots
1/4 cup white wine vinegar
8   5-inch-long fresh parsley stems
1 1/2 tablespoons fresh lemon juice
1   large fresh thyme sprig
2   fresh rosemary sprigs
1/4 cup heavy cream
3/4 cup (1 1/2 sticks) unsalted butter, cut into 12 pieces
    salt and pepper

For assembly:
4   tablespoons olive oil
1   carrot, peeled, cut into matchstick-size strips
1   red bell pepper, thinly sliced
6   cups thinly sliced Savoy cabbage

2   tablespoons (1/4 stick) unsalted butter

Garnish: chopped fresh chives and Mandarin orange slices

(Continued on next page)

Pecan-Crusted Trout with Orange-Rosemary Butter Sauce (continued)

Make trout:

Combine pecans and 1 tablespoon flour in food processor. Grind pecans finely; transfer to plate. Place remaining flour on another plate. Sprinkle fish with salt and pepper. Dip 1 fillet into flour to coat; shake off excess. Using pastry brush, brush flesh side with egg whites. Place fillet, egg white side down, onto pecans; press to coat with nuts. Transfer to waxed paper-lined baking sheet, pecan side down. Repeat with remaining 3 fillets; chill until nut crust is firm.

Make sauce:

Combine first 7 ingredients in medium saucepan. Boil 10 minutes; add rosemary. Boil until liquid is reduced to 1/2 cup, about 10 minutes. Strain sauce into another medium saucepan, pressing on solids in sieve. Add heavy cream; bring to boil. Reduce heat to medium-low. Whisk in butter 1 piece at a time (do not boil). Season with salt and pepper. Let stand at room temperature up to 2 hours.

To assemble:

Heat 2 tablespoons olive oil in heavy, large Dutch oven over high heat. Add carrot and bell pepper; toss 2 minutes. Add cabbage; toss until cabbage wilts, about 4 minutes. Season with salt and pepper. Remove from heat.

(Continued on next page)

Pecan-Crusted Trout with Orange-Rosemary Butter Sauce *(continued)*

Melt 1 tablespoon butter with 1 tablespoon oil in heavy large skillet over medium-high heat. Place 2 fillets, pecan side down, into skillet. Cook until crust is golden and crisp, about 2 minutes. Using spatula, turn fillets over. Cook until just opaque in center, about 2 minutes. Transfer to warmed platter. Repeat with remaining butter, oil and fish.

Whisk sauce over low heat to rewarm (do not boil). Divide vegetables among plates. Top with fish. Spoon sauce around fish and vegetables. Sprinkle with chopped chives and serve.

Riesling-Poached Trout with Thyme

Makes 4 servings

6	tablespoons (3/4 stick) chilled butter	4	trout, boned and butterflied salt and pepper
1	large leek (white and pale green parts only), thinly sliced	2	teaspoons minced fresh thyme
1	carrot, peeled, cut into matchstick-size strips	2	bay leaves, broken in half
		1	cup Johannisberg Riesling or other Riesling

Preheat oven to 450°F. Melt 1 tablespoon butter in heavy, large skillet over medium heat. Add sliced leek and carrot strips; sauté until crisp-tender, about 5 minutes. Remove from the heat.

Open fish flat and arrange skin side down in large roasting pan. Sprinkle fish with salt and pepper and 1 1/2 teaspoons of the minced fresh thyme. Top with leek and carrot mixture and bay leaves. Dot with 2 tablespoons butter. Pour Riesling over fish.

Bake fish until just opaque in center, about 15 minutes. Transfer fish and vegetables to warmed plates. Tent with foil to keep warm. Pour pan juices into heavy medium saucepan. Boil until reduced to 3/4 cup, about 6 minutes. Discard bay leaves. Add remaining 3 tablespoons butter and 1/2 teaspoon thyme and whisk just until butter is melted. Season to taste with salt and pepper. Pour sauce over fish and serve.

Trout with Lemon and Capers

Makes 2 to 4 servings

2	12-ounce trout, butterflied	2	tablespoons clarified butter or vegetable oil
1/2	cup all-purpose flour		
1	teaspoon salt	1	tablespoon unsalted butter
1/2	teaspoon freshly ground black pepper	1	lemon, juiced
		2	teaspoons salted capers, rinsed

Place flour in a shallow dish. Add salt and black pepper; stir with a fork to combine. Season butterflied trout lightly with more salt and pepper. Pat both sides of the trout in flour, shaking gently to remove excess flour.

Heat clarified butter or oil in a large skillet over medium-high heat. Add trout to skillet, skin-side up. Cook until pale golden, about 3 minutes. Turn and continue cooking, 3 to 4 minutes more.

Remove trout to a warmed serving platter. Remove skillet from heat. Add butter, lemon juice and capers. Brown the butter, stirring with a wooden spoon to release the brown bits in the bottom of the skillet, 1 to 2 minutes. Pour sauce over trout and serve immediately.

Chilled Pink Trout Filets with Basil Mayonnaise

Makes 6–8 servings

2	pounds pink trout filets		$1/2$	teaspoon salt
	water to cover		$1/4$	teaspoon white pepper
1	cup white wine vinegar			
2	shallots, diced			lettuce leaves, for platter
2	celery stalks, with leaves, coarsely chopped			basil leaves and cherry tomatoes for garnish

Place trout filets in skillet and cover with water. Add remaining ingredients (except lettuce and garnishes). Bring to a simmer and cook 5 to 6 minutes, or until fish is cooked through. Drain. Chill. At serving time, line a platter with lettuce leaves and place trout filet on lettuce. Top with Basil Mayonnaise. Garnish with basil leaves and cherry tomatoes.

Basil Mayonnaise:

1	clove garlic		2	tablespoons wine vinegar
$1/2$	cup basil leaves		1 to 2	cups canola or peanut oil
1	egg yolk		1	squirt of lemon
1	teaspoon salt		2	tablespoons capers
1	teaspoon dry mustard			

Put garlic and basil into container of blender. Blend on high until pulverized. Add egg yolk, salt, mustard and vinegar and turn blender on. When mixture is blended, start adding the oil, slowly through the feed tube, until mayonnaise thickens and comes together. Remove from blender. Stir in lemon and capers. Keep chilled until serving time.

Smoked Trout Canapés

Makes 36 canapes

1/2 pound smoked trout fillets, skinned, picked over and flaked

1/2 cup plain yogurt, drained in a fine sieve for 1 hour

1/4 cup mayonnaise

2 teaspoons fresh lemon juice

1 tablespoon minced fresh dill, plus dill sprigs for garnish

salt and pepper to taste

1 tablespoon minced onion, patted dry

12 slices of pumpernickel bread, each slice cut decoratively into 2-inch shapes

In a food processor, purée trout, yogurt, mayonnaise, lemon juice, minced dill, onion, and salt and pepper to taste until the mixture is smooth. The trout mixture may be made 1 day in advance and kept covered and chilled. On each piece of bread spread a scant teaspoon of the mixture, mounding it, and garnish each canapé with a small dill sprig.

Smoked Trout Horseradish Dip

Makes 2 cups

1/2 pound smoked trout or other smoked white fish

3/4 cup mayonnaise

1/2 cup sour cream

3 tablespoons chopped fresh dill leaves

2 tablespoons drained bottled horseradish, or to taste

Discard skin and bones from the smoked fish and break into pieces. In a food processor pulse fish until finely chopped. Stir in remaining ingredients and salt and pepper to taste. Serve dip with pumpernickel toasts or other crackers.

Sauces & Marinades

All-Purpose Wild Game Marinade

Makes 4 cups

1½ cups vegetable oil
⅓ cup minced red onion
¼ cup juniper berries, crushed
4 sprigs fresh rosemary
½ cup chopped parsley
2 tablespoons black peppercorns, cracked

1 cup red wine
3 cloves fresh garlic, chopped
3 shallots, chopped
½ cup red wine vinegar
¼ cup Worcestershire sauce
¼ cup soy sauce

Combine all ingredients. Use on any wild game. Marinate 12-24 hours, refrigerated.

Marinade for Alligator Steaks

Makes 2 cups

2 cups milk
2 teaspoons red pepper flakes

1 tablespoon fresh rosemary leaves

Combine all ingredients. Pour over alligator steaks and refrigerate. Marinate 4-8 hours.

Bulgogi Marinade

Makes 2 cups

1 cup soy sauce
½ cup water
3 tablespoons green onion, chopped
3 teaspoons garlic, crushed
1 tablespoon sugar

3 teaspoons fresh ginger, minced
1 tablespoon black pepper
2 tablespoons sesame seeds, toasted and ground
2 tablespoons olive oil

Blend all ingredients for marinade. Place meat cubes in marinade for 8 to 24 hours, refrigerated. Use for venison, duck, or wild boar.

Venison Steak Marinade

Makes 3 cups

¼	cup juniper berries, crushed	3	cloves garlic, crushed
4	sprigs fresh rosemary	3	shallots, chopped
2	tablespoons black peppercorns, crushed	1½	cups Italian dressing
		½	cup A-1® Steak Sauce
1	cup red wine	½	cup soy sauce

Combine the marinade ingredients and pour over the venison steaks in shallow dish to cover completely. Wrap tightly with plastic or foil and place in refrigerator for at least 24 hours.

Venison Stir-Fry Marinade

Makes ½ cup

3	tablespoons soy sauce	1	teaspoon sugar
2	tablespoons sake or dry white wine	1	teaspoon black pepper
1	teaspoon ginger	1	tablespoon crushed black peppercorns
2	tablespoons cornstarch		

Mix the marinade ingredients in a casserole. Add the meat, stir to coat the meat well. Let marinate at least 1 hour, turning frequently.

If marinating for more than 1 hour, refrigerate. Enough to marinate 1 pound of venison, boar or elk, cut small for stir-fry.

Quail Marinade

Makes ¾ cup

¼ cup olive oil
2 garlic cloves, minced
2 tablespoons white wine

2 tablespoons soy sauce
2 tablespoons ginger, ground or fresh

Blend all ingredients. Pour over quail. Cover and refrigerate 8 to 12 hours or overnight.

Shish Kabunny Marinade

Makes 1 cup

¼ cup vegetable oil
½ cup onion, chopped
¼ cup cilantro, chopped

¼ cup lemon juice
1 teaspoon Italian seasoning
1 clove garlic, minced

Combine all ingredients and pour over rabbit. Cover and marinate at least 12 hours, refrigerated.

Rabbit Marinade

Makes 1 ½ quarts

2 cups red wine
2 cups chicken broth
2 teaspoons allspice
2 bay leaves

1 teaspoon thyme
1 teaspoon ground cumin
½ cup canola oil

Combine all ingredients and pour over rabbit. Cover and marinate, refrigerated, 24 hours. May be reduced in direct proportion.

Diener Rabbit Marinade

Makes 3 cups

½	cup vinegar	4	whole juniper berries, crushed
½	cup water		
1	cup dry red wine	1	bay leaf
1	large onion, sliced	4	whole cloves
10	whole peppercorns, crushed	½	tablespoon pickling spice

Place rabbit pieces and giblets in a deep bowl. Combine marinade ingredients in medium pot and simmer 15 minutes. Cook marinade and pour over the rabbit. Cover and marinate in refrigerator 1 to 2 days, turning meat once or twice each day.

Jalapeño Marinade

Makes 1 cup

1	tablespoon olive oil	1	tablespoon kosher salt
¼	cup red wine	3	tablespoons cracked pepper
1	tablespoon Worcestershire sauce	3	tablespoons garlic, minced
1	teaspoon fresh thyme, chopped	3	tablespoons cayenne pepper

Whisk together the marinade ingredients and cover both sides of venison steaks or elk chops with the mixture. Cover and allow to marinate in the refrigerator for 6 to 12 hours.

Jicama and Roasted Red Pepper Sauce

Makes 2 cups

1	cup peeled jicama in ¼-inch dice	1	poblano chili, seeded and diced
4	red peppers, roasted and diced	1	cup beef stock
1	teaspoon shallot, chopped	3	tablespoons cold, heavy cream
1	teaspoon garlic, minced	¼	cup sour cream
			salt and pepper to taste

Place jicama, red peppers, shallots, garlic, chili and beef stock in a sauté pan. Bring to a boil and simmer until almost all liquid is evaporated. Place mixture into food processor or blender and puree. Remove and place in saucepan on low heat or in double boiler. Add heavy cream, sour cream, salt and pepper to taste and blend. Serve with game ravioli or grilled duck breast.

* To roast peppers, place directly over open gas flame, turning frequently until blackened. Or place peppers on a pan and broil in oven until blackened. Placed blackened peppers in a paper bag for 10-15 minutes. Peel off blackened skin, remove seeds and stem, and cut roasted peppers into dice.

BBQ Dipping Sauce

Makes 2 cups

½ cup ketchup
¼ cup apple cider vinegar
½ cup vegetable oil
2 tablespoons light brown sugar
½ envelope dry onion soup mix
1 tablespoon stone-ground mustard

1 teaspoon prepared horseradish
¼ teaspoon garlic powder
½ cup water
1 tablespoon liquid Barbecue Smoke®
1 tablespoon Tabasco® sauce, or to taste

Combine all ingredients in a small saucepan; bring to a boil; lower heat and simmer about 10 minutes. Cool before using. May be made a day ahead. Reheat before serving. Serve with any batter-fried or grilled wild game.

Creolaise Dipping Sauce

Makes 1 cup

2 egg yolks
1 tablespoon fresh lemon juice
⅓ teaspoon salt
⅛ teaspoon cayenne
2 teaspoons water

1 stick butter, melted and warm
1 tablespoon whole grain Creole mustard
2 teaspoons parsley, finely chopped

This is a basic hollandaise sauce, modified with Creole seasonings. In a double boiler or stainless steel bowl set over a pot of simmering water on medium heat, whisk the egg yolks with lemon juice, salt, cayenne and water until pale yellow and slightly thick. (Be careful not to let the bowl touch the water, as it might get too hot and set the eggs.) As soon as the eggs begin to thicken, remove the bowl from the pot and, whisking quickly, add the butter, 1 teaspoon at a time, until well blended. Add the creole mustard and chopped parsley. Serve immediately. Goes well with frog legs, grilled trout or quail. Can replace traditional Hollandaise sauce in any dish.

Indonesian Peanut Dipping Sauce

Makes 1 ¼ cups

1   clove garlic, minced
1   tablespoon peanut oil
1   teaspoon red chile peppers, dried/soaked
2   teaspoons tamarind, dissolved in 2 tablespoons water

1   teaspoon salt
2   tablespoons sugar
1   cup smooth peanut butter

This dipping sauce can be made one day ahead. Sauté the garlic in peanut oil until light brown. Add chile peppers, tamarind liquid, salt and sugar. When mixture starts to simmer, add peanut butter until blended. Store at room temperature. Serve with boar satay or rabbit kabobs.

Jalapeño Sauce

Makes 3 cups

22 jalapeños, stemmed, cut crosswise, seeded (about 2 cups)
3   cloves garlic, sliced
½   cup thinly sliced onion

¾   teaspoon salt
1   tablespoon sugar
1   teaspoon vegetable oil
2   cups water
1   cup apple cider vinegar

Combine the jalapeños, garlic, onions, salt, sugar and oil in saucepan over high heat. Sauté for 3 to 5 minutes. Add water and continue to cook stirring often, for about 2 minutes. Remove from the heat and allow to steep until mixture cools completely. Once cooled, puree the mixture in a food processor for 15 to 20 seconds, or until very smooth. With the processor running, pour the vinegar through the feed tube in a steady stream. Pour into a sterilized jar and secure with airtight lid. Refrigerate. Best if aged 2 to 3 weeks before using. May be stored up to 4 months in the refrigerator. A great condiment to serve with any wild game.

Orange Sauce

Makes 3 cups

8 cups duck or game broth
1 tablespoon cornstarch
2 tablespoons cold water
⅓ cup Mandarin orange segments, cut in half
¼ cup brandy or Cognac
½ cup sugar

¼ cup orange juice
¼ cup cider vinegar
1 tablespoon Mandarin orange jam
   salt and freshly ground pepper to taste

Place the broth in a large saucepan and simmer over medium heat until reduced to 2½ cups. Combine the cornstarch and cold water in a small bowl and mix well. Add this mixture to the reduced broth, whisking constantly. Simmer 1 to 2 minutes, or until the broth is thickened and set aside and keep warm. Combine the Mandarin oranges with the brandy, set aside. Combine the sugar and 1 teaspoon of the orange juice in a medium sauté pan and cook over medium heat without stirring. Once the sugar has begun to melt, stir occasionally until the sugar is completely melted and golden brown, about 8 minutes. Immediately add the vinegar and continue to cook until reduced by half. Add the remaining orange juice to the reduced sugar, drain the brandy from the oranges and add it to the orange juice mixture. Simmer until reduced by half. Add the thickened broth, Mandarin orange pieces and preserves. Blend, adding the salt and pepper to taste. Set sauce aside and keep warm before serving with duck, quail or pheasant.

Raisin Apricot Sauce

Makes 1 ½ cups

1	10-ounce jar apricot jam	½	cup raisins
½	cup water	1	teaspoon cinnamon
¼	cup butter	1	teaspoon ground cloves

In a small saucepan combine jam with water, stir over low heat until well combined, add butter, cinnamon, cloves, raisins. Cook until butter is melted and sauce begins to bubble. In blender puree mixture and glaze quail or other game bird.

Ranchero Sauce

Makes 2 ½ cups

2	cups tomatoes, chopped	¼	teaspoon pepper
¼	cup water	¼	teaspoon sugar
1	tablespoon onions, chopped	¼	teaspoon ground cumin
1	tablespoon garlic, crushed	⅓	cup cilantro, chopped
½	teaspoon salt		

Cook the tomatoes and water uncovered over medium heat until tomatoes soften. Mash tomatoes, add onions, garlic and spices and stir until well blended. Remove any tomato skins. Just before serving add the cilantro. Serve warm over game burritos or with other Tex-Mex game dishes.

Sauce Mexicana

Makes 4 ½ cups

¾	cup vegetable oil		salt to taste
4	dried chipotle peppers	25	tomatillos, fresh or canned
1	dried ancho chile	½	cup fresh cilantro, chopped
2	white onions, peeled and quartered	⅓	cup olive oil
4	medium garlic cloves	2	thick onion slices

Heat vegetable oil over medium heat in large skillet. Sauté chipotles and ancho briefly to soften—approximately 3 minutes. Remove peppers/chiles and drain. In same pan, add onions and garlic and brown, adding a pinch or two of salt. If using fresh tomatillos, remove the papery husks. In blender or food processor, puree tomatillos. Add mixture from skillet and puree again. Add cilantro and pulse several times. You may have to puree mixture in batches. Reserve sauce.

In large saucepan, heat olive oil and brown the two thick onion slices until browned to season the pan. Remove onions and discard (or save for another use). Add sauce to the pan and cook over low heat for 30 to 45 minutes to blend all flavors. Correct seasoning, adding salt and pepper to taste. Good with wild game burritos or enchiladas. Extra sauce will keep refrigerated a few days or may be frozen.

Sherry Wine Sauce

Makes 6 cups

¾ cup bacon, diced
3 tablespoons olive oil
3 tablespoons butter
1½ cups carrots, peeled and
   diced
1½ cups onion, diced
1 cup leeks, diced
½ cup celery, sliced
1 head garlic, cut in half
   crosswise with skin

1 cup sherry wine vinegar
1 cup sherry
3 cups chicken stock
12 black peppercorns
½ cup cumin seeds, roasted
2 dried ancho chili peppers,
   toasted and seeded
2 dried chipotle chili peppers,
   toasted and seeded
1 bay leaf, crushed

In a medium saucepan, on medium heat add together the bacon fat, oil and butter. Cook 3 to 5 minutes, or until browned. Add carrot, onion, leeks, celery and garlic and cook until vegetables are softened. Add vinegar and wine, reduce to half. Add stock, peppercorns, cumin seeds, chili peppers and bay leaf. Reduce to half again until you have a light sauce. Strain and reserve. If a thicker sauce is desired, mix a little cornstarch and water together, add to and bring to a boil to thicken. Good with duck or pheasant. Extra sauce keeps several days in refrigerator or may be frozen.

Apricot Fig Sauce

Makes 6 cups

Step 1:

1	goose carcass or 2 to 3 duck carcasses	2	tablespoons tomato paste
2	large onions, quartered	½	cup bacon drippings
2	large carrots, quartered	2	cups red wine
2	medium parsnips, quartered	1	bay leaf
1	medium rutabaga, quartered	½	teaspoon juniper berries
8	shallots, whole	3 to 4	garlic cloves, sliced
1	cup celery, chopped	2	teaspoons thyme, dried

Preheat oven to 400°. Cut up carcass(es) and combine in large roasting pan with onions, carrots, parsnips, rutabaga, shallots, celery, tomato paste and bacon drippings. Place in oven and roast until brown, about 30 minutes, stirring occasionally. Save shallots for final sauce preparation. Transfer bones and vegetables to large stockpot. Add wine, bay leaf, juniper berries, garlic and thyme. Add enough cold water to cover by ⅓. Bring to a boil and immediately reduce heat to low simmer. This will insure a clear sauce. Do not let sit once boiled. Cook until water is reduced by half. Strain all juice out and place in a separate pan to reduce slowly to ⅓ of volume.

(Continued on next page)

Apricot Fig Sauce (continued)

Step 2:

3	cups white balsamic vinegar	8	oven-roasted shallots
2	cups port or red wine	1	stick softened butter
8	figs, slivered	1	teaspoon fresh sage, chopped
10	ripe or canned apricot halves	1	teaspoon tarragon, chopped

Reduce balsamic vinegar and wine in pan until almost syrupy. The flavor should be sweet and sour, but not bitter. Add figs, apricots and reserved shallots and simmer 5 minutes to blend flavors. Combine the wine and stock reductions and adjust seasonings. Gently add the softened butter and herbs. Serve over goose, duck or other game birds. Extra sauce may be frozen.

Banana Rum Sauce

Makes 1 ½ cups

4	tablespoons butter	¼	cup light corn syrup
2	tablespoons sugar	3	tablespoons dark rum
1	tablespoon cornstarch	1	tablespoon banana extract
¾	cup milk		

Melt butter in a small saucepan, combine sugar and cornstarch, add to butter. Stir in milk and corn syrup. Cook and stir over medium heat until the mixture comes to a full boil. Boil for 1 minute. Remove from heat and stir in dark rum and banana extract. Serve warm sauce over bread pudding or ice cream.

Seasonings, Relishes, Sides and Accompaniments

Pear, Apple & Ginger Chutney

Makes 6 cups

4	Granny Smith apples	10	peppercorns
3	Anjou pears	½	teaspoon allspice berries
1¼	cups honey	⅔	cup diced candied ginger
¾	cup cider vinegar	½	cup stemmed maraschino
⅓	cup white balsamic vinegar		cherries, cut in half
5	whole cloves		

Peel and core the apples and pears; then cut into very small pieces. Place in a pot with the rest of the ingredients except the candied ginger and cherries. Bring contents of pot to a boil. Simmer until fruits are soft, about 15 minutes. Stir in the candied ginger and maraschino cherries and simmer 2 to 3 minutes. Pour chutney into a clean, heat proof bowl, cover and refrigerate several hours before serving.

Goes well with boar, quail, elk, duck and other wild game.

This chutney will keep well in the refrigerator for several weeks. If desired, instead of chilling after cooking, you can pour the chutney into 6 sterilized jars, cap with lids and rings and place in a boiling water bath for 10 minutes.

These are handy gifts, as well.

Green Tomato Relish

Makes 6 pints

3	pounds green tomatoes	2 to 3 stalks celery	
1	pound yellow onions (about 2-3 large)	2	bags slaw mix, with carrot
		1½	teaspoons turmeric
1	red bell pepper	2	cups white vinegar
1	green bell pepper	2¼	cups sugar, or to taste
1 to 2 hot peppers		Salt to taste	

Cut the green tomatoes, onions peppers and celery very fine, but do not mince. If using a food processor, be careful not to over-process. The vegetables should not be pureed. Place vegetables in a large pot. Stir in the slaw mix, turmeric, vinegar, and sugar, and combine well. Bring mixture to a simmer, but do not boil. Stir in salt to taste. Mix again. Then, ladle into sterilized pint jars, top with lids and rings. Place filled jars in boiling water bath for 10 minutes. Carefully remove jars and let cool.

Good with wild boar, quail, and pheasant.

Blackening Seasoning

Makes 2¾ cups

3	tablespoons dried thyme	5	tablespoons ground black pepper
3	tablespoons dried oregano		
6	tablespoons garlic powder	2	tablespoons red pepper flakes, minced
4	tablespoons cayenne pepper		

Combine all ingredients in a mixing bowl. Blend well. Can be stored up to 3 months in an air tight container in pantry. Use on Alligator Steaks, Venison Steaks, trout or any pan-grilled game.

West Indian Masala

Makes ⅔ cup

6	tablespoons coriander seeds	1½	teaspoons cumin seeds
1	teaspoon fenugreek seeds	2	teaspoons ground turmeric
2	tablespoons fennel seeds	1	teaspoon ground Jamaican
1	teaspoon mustard seeds		allspice, or other allspice

Preheat oven to 350°. Spread all seeds on a sheet pan or cookie sheet. Roast until seeds start to pop. Shake pan and cover with additional sheet pan. Continue to roast 8 to 10 minutes more, shaking pan occasionally. Be careful not to let seeds burn! Cool slightly, then grind all the seeds in a spice mill or blender. Add turmeric and allspice, blend well. Unused masala can be stored in a tightly covered jar. Use on squirrel, goat, quail or rabbit.

Blueberry Pecan Relish

Makes 3½ cups

1	orange	2	cups fresh or frozen
½	lemon		blueberries
½	lime	½	cup pecans, chopped
¼	cup granulated sugar	2	tablespoons brandy or
			Cognac

Quarter and seed the oranges, lemon, and lime keeping the peels on. Place citrus fruit and sugar in food processor and process with on/off turns to coarsely chop, but not puree. Add the blueberries and quickly process again with a few on/off turns to make a relish. Place fruit mixture in bowl; add chopped pecans and Cognac. Stir well, and refrigerate at least 1 hour before serving to allow flavors to blend. Remember, this is a relish, not a sauce! Top any baked or grilled game such as wild boar chops or venison with this relish.

Bing Cherry Relish

Makes 3 cups

1½ cups bing cherries, pitted
½ medium red onion, diced
½ medium green onion, sliced
½ medium green bell pepper, chopped
½ medium jalapeño pepper, seeded and minced (leave seeds in if you like it hot!)
3 tablespoons raisins, plumped

1 tablespoon cilantro, finely chopped
1 teaspoon orange zest, finely chopped
⅓ cup orange juice
1 tablespoon Dijon mustard
1½ teaspoons ground cumin
¼ cup canola oil
salt to taste

In large bowl, combine cherries, red onion, green onion, bell pepper, jalapeño pepper, raisins, cilantro and orange zest. In a food processor or blender, combine orange juice, mustard and cumin until smooth. With the machine running, gradually add the oil in a very thin stream; mixture will thicken. Pour dressing over the cherry mixture. Toss gently. Season to taste with salt. Cover and refrigerate at least 2 to 4 hours before serving. Serve with grilled venison or boar chops.

Sun-Dried Tomato and Corn Salsa

Makes 3 cups

1	cup sun-dried tomatoes	3	serrano peppers, seeded and
	water to cover		minced
4	tablespoons onion, finely	4	tablespoons cilantro, minced
	chopped	2	tablespoons lemon or lime
2	cloves garlic, minced		juice
2	cups boiling water		salt and pepper to taste
2	large ripe tomatoes, chopped	½	cup whole kernel cooked or
			roasted corn

Soak sun-dried tomatoes in warm water until soft; drain and chop. Put chopped onion and garlic into a fine strainer and pour 2 cups of boiling water over them; drain thoroughly. Let cool. Combine sun-dried tomatoes, fresh tomatoes, peppers, cilantro and lemon juice with the onions and garlic, adding salt and pepper to taste. Add roasted corn kernels and refrigerate to allow flavors to blend. Serve with venison or elk or with tortilla chips.

Chipotle Mayonnaise

Makes 1 ½ cups

1   cup mayonnaise
6   ounces chipotle peppers canned in adobo sauce

Puree canned chipotles in adobo sauce, add 1 cup of mayonnaise, stir well. Store in the refrigerator in a covered jar or container until needed. (You can store Chipotle Mayonnaise up to a week.) Use on venison, buffalo burgers or for game meat sandwiches.

Honey and Chili Glaze

Makes 1 cup

2   tablespoons olive oil
6   cloves garlic, chopped
1   poblano chili, seeded, deveined and julienned
1   ancho chili, toasted in a dry skillet, soaked in warm water to soften, drained and then rough chopped

3   tablespoons sherry wine vinegar
½   cup honey
    salt and pepper to taste

Heat oil, add garlic and peppers and sauté for 3 minutes. Add vinegar and reduce by half. Add honey. Remove from heat, allow to steep. Strain; season to taste and cool. Brush on quail or other wild game before grilling.

Polenta

Makes 4 servings

4	cups chicken broth	½	cup parmesan cheese,
½	teaspoon coarse salt		freshly grated
½	cup cornmeal	2	tablespoons unsalted butter
½	cup semolina		

Heat the chicken stock and salt in a 2-quart saucepan over medium heat until almost boiling. Reduce the heat to simmer, mix together the cornmeal and semolina, and slowly stir in into the hot stock, stirring constantly with a wire whisk. To avoid lumps, continue stirring until all the polenta has been added and the mixture begins to thicken, 20 to 25 minutes. Remove from the heat. Stir in the cheese and butter and season with salt as needed. Immediately pour into baking dish. Serve hot. Instant polentas are also available in most grocery stores. Good with game birds.

Spaetzle

Makes 6 servings

2¼	cups flour	2	whole eggs
¼	teaspoon nutmeg	¼	teaspoon baking powder
1	teaspoon salt	1	cup milk

Fill a 4 to 6 quart pot with water. Add a little salt and bring to a boil.

Sift together the flour, salt, baking powder and nutmeg. Add eggs and mix. Add milk gradually, beating vigorously to trap air until the batter is stiff, but smooth. Press dough flat on a plate or floured board. With a sharp knife, scrape small pieces of dough off and drop into rapidly boiling water. There should only be one layer of spaetzle at a time in the cooking water. Boil gently 3 to 5 minutes or until you try a few and find them done and floating. Good with hasenpfeffer.

Egg Pasta Dough

Makes 6 servings

2⅓ cups all-purpose flour, plus   3   extra-large eggs
½ cup for board and extra
for sprinkling

Hand Method: Heap the 2⅓ cups of flour on a clean, floured surface, making a well in the center. Break the eggs into the well, and using a fork or your fingers, combine the eggs with the flour in a circular motion, until all of the eggs are combined with the flour. Continue to knead until smooth. Place a damp towel over the pasta dough and let rest for 20 minutes. Pull off a piece of dough the size of an egg. Roll out until very thin. Cut into fettuccine or other pasta shapes by hand or use a pasta wheel. Let dry slightly before boiling.

Food Processor Method: Place the flour into the container of a food processor. With the motor running, add the eggs one at a time. When the dough forms a ball on the blade, remove it and let rest for 30 minutes. Roll out using a hand-crank pasta rolling machine.

Good as an accompaniment to any wild game dish that has a sauce.

Jalapeño Orange Butter

Makes ⅔ cup

¼ cup unsalted butter, room
temperature
⅛ cup orange marmalade with
zest, room temperature

2 tablespoons canned
jalapeno, minced
2 tablespoons fresh cilantro,
coarsely chopped

Stir together the butter and and marmalade. Add the jalapeño and
cilantro. Portion into tablespoon-size servings and refrigerate. This can
be made 2 days ahead. Serve on grilled venison steaks or duck breasts.

Desserts

Apple Crumb Pie

Makes 6–8 servings

1	9-inch pastry pie shell	1	cup packed brown sugar
6	cooking apples	½	teaspoon ground cinnamon
2	teaspoons lemon juice	½	teaspoon ground ginger
½	cup sugar	¼	teaspoon ground allspice
1	cup all-purpose flour	½	cup butter

Pare apples, cut into eighths and remove all core.

Sprinkle with lemon juice while placing in mixing bowl. When all apples are prepared, sprinkle with ½ cup sugar, tossing to mix all. Preheat oven to 400°F. Arrange apples in unbaked pie shell. Mix together flour, brown sugar and all spices; cut in the butter until crumbly. Spoon evenly over apples. Bake 40 to 45 minutes. This is an open-faced pie, though if desired, you may top with additional pastry.

Apple Raspberry Strudel

Makes 8 servings

3	medium Golden Delicious apples		pinch salt
¾	cup fresh breadcrumbs	6	sheets phyllo dough
⅓	cup sugar	½	cup butter, melted
½	teaspoon ginger	½	cup raspberries, fresh or frozen
½	teaspoon cinnamon		powdered sugar

Preheat oven 375°. Thaw phyllo, keeping a towel on top to keep moist.

Wash, peel and core apples. Cut in half and then thinly slice.

In large mixing bowl, add breadcrumbs, sugar, ginger, cinnamon and salt. Blend well.

Butter a cookie sheet or spray with nonstick spray. Line your work surface with wax paper. Lay one phyllo sheet on top of wax paper. Brush phyllo sheet with butter and sprinkle about 1 teaspoon of breadcrumbs over sheet. Repeat with next 5 remaining sheets, ending with breadcrumbs. Lengthwise of the dough place ½ of the apple mixture, then put raspberries down center and finally another row of the remaining apple mixture. Fold ends over filling, roll up jelly roll fashion starting at long edge near filling. You may need to tuck in apples to make a 3-inch wide roll. Put strudel roll seam side down on baking sheet. Brush top with butter. Bake 40 minutes, until golden.

Let rest 5 to 8 minutes, slice thickly and sprinkle with powder sugar. To rewarm, bake 10 to 15 minutes at 300°. It's best not to microwave it.

Strudel can be made 1 week ahead and frozen. Do not thaw strudel before baking. If frozen, bake approximately 50 minutes at 375°.

Baked Apples

Makes 4 servings

1	cup unsweetened apple juice	¼	teaspoon cinnamon
¼	cup raisins	¼	teaspoon allspice
1	cinnamon stick	¼	teaspoon ginger
4	large apples	¼	cup sliced almonds
1	teaspoon lemon juice		fresh whipped cream
2	tablespoons honey		

Combine apple juice, raisins and cinnamon stick in a heavy saucepan. Cook over low heat until mixture begins to boil. Remove from heat and let steep for 30 minutes. Strain juice into small bowl. Reserve raisins and throw out cinnamon stick.

Preheat oven to 400°. Core apples and peel 1 inch from tops. Place apples in pie plate. Drain raisins, reserving apple juice. Spoon raisins into hollows of apples. Bake until apples are just tender, basting with reserved apple juice, approximately 20 minutes. Combine lemon juice, honey and spices. Pour over apples and continue to bake until apples are very tender, but do not lose their shape, about 10 more minutes. Sprinkle with sliced almonds and bake until almonds are toasted, about 3 minutes more. Serve warm or at room temperature with fresh whipped cream.

Banana Bread Pudding with Banana Rum Sauce

Makes 6 servings

4	cups day-old French bread, cubed	3	teaspoons vanilla extract
		1	teaspoon ground cinnamon
¼	cup butter, melted	½	teaspoon ground nutmeg
3	eggs	½	teaspoon salt
2	cups milk	1	cup firm bananas, sliced
½	cup sugar		

Preheat oven to 375°.

Place the bread cubes in a greased 2 quart casserole; pour butter over and toss to coat. In a medium bowl, lightly beat eggs, then beat in milk, sugar, vanilla, cinnamon, nutmeg and salt. Stir in bananas. Pour over bread cubes and stir to coat. Bake uncovered at for 40 minutes or until knife inserted comes out clean. While pudding is baking, prepare banana rum sauce.

Banana Rum Sauce

Makes 6 servings

4	tablespoons butter	3	tablespoons dark rum
2	tablespoons sugar	1	tablespoon banana extract
1	tablespoon cornstarch		
¾	cup milk		
¼	cup light corn syrup		

Melt butter in a small saucepan, combine sugar and cornstarch, add to butter. Stir in milk and corn syrup. Cook and stir over medium heat until the mixture comes to a full boil. Boil for 1 minute. Remove from heat and stir in dark rum and banana extract. Serve warm sauce over bread pudding.

Blueberry Nut Cobbler

Makes 6-8 servings

3	cups self-rising cake flour	½	cup walnuts, chopped
¾	cup unsalted butter	½	teaspoon ground nutmeg
1 to 1¼	cups buttermilk	1	teaspoon ground cinnamon
3	pints blueberries, rinsed and cleaned	3	tablespoons unsalted butter buttermilk for brushing
¾	cup sugar		sugar for sprinkling
2	teaspoons lemon zest, finely grated		

For the cobbler top: Place flour in a bowl and incorporate butter until fine and mealy. Do not allow to become pasty. Stir in 1 cup of the buttermilk, add the remaining buttermilk only if mixture seems too dry. Press dough together on a floured surface, wrap and allow to rest while preparing filling.

For the filling: Preheat oven to 450° and set rack in the middle of the oven. Place blueberries in a bowl and add sugar, lemon zest, chopped walnuts, nutmeg and cinnamon. Toss well to combine and pour filling into a 2 quart baking dish. Distribute pieces of the butter evenly on the filling.

Press or roll out cobbler top, slide the pastry dough on top of the baking dish, on top of the filling. Cut 3 or 4 vent holes in the crust. Brush the top of the pastry with buttermilk and sprinkle with sugar. Bake the cobbler about 20 minutes, until crust is well browned and filling is bubbly.

Bourbon Pecan Pie

Makes 6–8 servings

1	9-inch unbaked pie crust	1	teaspoon butter, melted
	foil	4	tablespoons flour
	dry beans or pennies, to	½	teaspoon salt
	weight pie shell	1	teaspoon vanilla extract
3	eggs	½	teaspoon cinnamon
1	cup brown sugar	2	cups pecans
1	cup corn syrup		whipped cream
¼	cup bourbon		cinnamon for garnish

Preheat the oven to 350°. Bake the pie crust, lined with foil and dry beans or pennies for 8 to 10 minutes, just long enough to dry it out. Do not let it brown. Cool a few minutes, then remove foil and weights. Meanwhile, beat the eggs. Add the sugar, syrup, bourbon, butter, flour, salt, vanilla, cinnamon and pecans. Pour into pie crust and bake for about 1 hour or until pie is firm in the middle and edge of crust is brown. If crust is browning too fast, wrap foil around it.

Bread Pudding with Bourbon Sauce

Makes 10 servings

8	cups loosely packed torn stale bread of your choice (you can use left over muffins, French bread, etc.)	2	teaspoons vanilla extract
		1	cup sugar
		1	teaspoon cinnamon
		½	teaspoon nutmeg
6	egg yolks	¾	stick butter, cut into small pieces
6	cups milk		

Place the bread pieces in a large casserole. Combine the egg yolks, milk, vanilla, sugar, cinnamon and nutmeg and whisk until the sugar dissolves. Pour the mixture over the bread and let stand 30 minutes, mashing down occasionally. Preheat the oven to 300°. Dot the top of bread mixture with butter and place casserole in larger roasting pan. Fill roasting pan with enough water to come halfway up the sides of the baking dish. Place in oven and bake until the pudding sets and a knife inserted into the center comes out clean. Remove pudding from the oven and discard water bath. Serve pudding lukewarm or at room temperature, topped with Bourbon Sauce.

Bourbon Sauce:

½	stick butter	½	teaspoon cinnamon
½	cup sugar	4	egg yolks, beaten
¼	cup bourbon		

Melt the butter in top of a double boiler over simmering water. Add the sugar and whisk to dissolve. Add the bourbon and cinnamon and whisk for 1 to 2 minutes. Remove from the heat and drizzle in the egg yolks, whisking constantly. Place pot over simmering water again, and continue whisking until the sauce is pale and slightly thickened, 3 to 5 minutes. Spoon Bourbon Sauce over pudding and serve immediately.

Carrot Cake

Makes 10 servings

1½	cups vegetable oil	2	cups cake flour
2	cups light brown sugar	2	teaspoons baking powder
4	large eggs	1½	teaspoons baking soda
2	cups carrots, shredded	½	teaspoon salt
1	8½-ounce can crushed pineapple, drained	3	teaspoons cinnamon

Icing:

1	8-ounce package cream cheese	½	stick butter
¼	cup honey	2	teaspoons vanilla
			pecan pieces, optional

Preheat oven to 350°. Grease and flour tube or bundt pan.

In large mixing bowl, mix oil and sugar, then add one egg at a time, until smooth. Add carrots and pineapple and blend. Sift flour, baking powder, baking soda, salt and cinnamon. Blend with carrot mixture. Pour into tube or bundt pan and bake 1 hour.

Icing: When cake is cool, add the frosting. Mix together in small mixing bowl, softened cream cheese, honey, butter and vanilla. Spread over cake as desired. May garnish with optional pecan pieces.

Cherry or Peach Cobbler

Makes 4-6 servings

Filling:

5 cups pitted cherries or diced peaches, canned or fresh	¼ teaspoon ground nutmeg
	¼ cup water, if using fresh fruit
2½ tablespoons lemon juice	1 tablespoon vanilla extract, if
⅓ cup granulated sugar	using peaches
⅓ cup brown sugar, packed	1 teaspoon almond extract, if
2½ tablespoons cornstarch	using cherries
1 teaspoon ground cinnamon	¼ teaspoon ground ginger

Preheat oven to 425°. Toss fruit with lemon juice and set aside. If using canned fruit, drain, reserving ¼ cup juice. In a saucepan, combine sugars, cornstarch, cinnamon, nutmeg and the reserved fruit juice or water. Bring to a boil, stirring frequently about 2 minutes. Remove from heat and add fruit and flavoring. Pour into an ungreased 8-inch square baking pan.

Topping:

2 cups all-purpose flour	½ teaspoon salt
2 tablespoons granulated sugar	2 tablespoons butter
	1 cup milk, approximately
2 teaspoons baking powder	

Combine flour, sugar, baking powder and salt; cut in butter until crumbly. Stir in enough milk to moisten, but dough should not be runny. Drop by tablespoonfuls over fruit mixture.

Bake for 25 to 30 minutes or until golden brown. If the fruit is very juicy, it will have to be baked longer. If desired, serve topped with ice cream or whipped cream.

Note: This recipe may be doubled.

Chocolate Cherries Jubilee

Makes 4 servings

1	cup cherry preserves or cherry pie filling	6	tablespoons Cognac or brandy
¼	teaspoon cinnamon	1	pint chocolate-chocolate-chip ice cream
⅛	teaspoon nutmeg	¼	cup toasted almonds

Melt preserves or heat cherry pie filling in heavy small saucepan over low heat, stirring frequently. Mix in cinnamon and nutmeg and 2 tablespoons of Cognac. Place remaining Cognac in separate small saucepan or scoop-neck metal gravy boat.

Scoop ice cream into 4 bowls, spoon sauce over, garnish with almonds. With a long match or lighter, light Cognac in saucepan or gravy boat to flame and pour over each individual bowl. Serve immediately. Be very careful not to burn yourself or your guests if flaming at the table. This is a great finish to a meal and is quite showy!

Custard Fruit Pie

Makes 8 servings

1	large 10-inch pie shell, unbaked and chilled	2½	cups milk, scalded
½	cup sugar	1	cup coconut flakes
1	teaspoon all-purpose flour	¾	cup fresh washed raspberries, blueberries, or strawberries
¼	teaspoon salt		plus additional berries for garnishing
4	eggs, slightly beaten		
1½	teaspoons vanilla extract		

Preheat oven to 400°. Mix sugar, flour and salt together in a bowl. Stir in eggs and vanilla extract. Gradually add hot milk, beating to mix well, stir in coconut. Remove chilled pie crust from refrigerator. Place fruit

(Continued on next page)

Custard Fruit Pie *(Continued from previous page)*

on bottom of shell. Pour custard over fruit. Bake for 35 to 40 minutes or until a knife inserted in center of pie comes out clean. Remove pie from oven and let cool at room temperature. Place in refrigerator several hours before serving. Garnish with fresh berries.

German Chocolate Pie

Makes 6–8 servings

1	9-inch frozen pie crust	¼	cup hot water
2	tablespoons cocoa	2	large eggs
1	teaspoon cornstarch	1	cup evaporated milk
2	tablespoons all-purpose flour	2	tablespoons Hershey's® chocolate syrup
¼	teaspoon salt	⅔	cup coconut, shredded
1	tablespoon butter, softened	1	cup pecan pieces

Preheat oven to 350°.

Combine dry ingredients. Add butter and water, mix well. Add eggs, milk, syrup, coconut and pecans, mix well.

Pour into unbaked pie crust. Bake until center is firm, approximately 20 to 30 minutes. If crust is browning too quickly, cover edges in foil.

Kahlua Brownies

Makes 12 servings

2	ounces chocolate, unsweetened	1	teaspoon vanilla
¼	cup butter plus 1 teaspoon for greasing pan	1	tablespoon instant coffee crystals
1	cup all-purpose flour	3	tablespoons Kahlua
1	cup sugar	½	teaspoon salt
2	eggs, well beaten	½	teaspoon baking powder

Icing:

2	ounces chocolate, unsweetened and chopped	¼	teaspoon salt
1½	cups sugar	1	teaspoon vanilla
7	tablespoons milk		chocolate chips or chocolate shavings for garnish
¼	cup butter	2	tablespoons Kahlua
1	tablespoon light corn syrup		

Preheat oven to 350°.

Brownies: Melt chocolate and butter in top of double boiler over simmering water. Remove chocolate mixture from heat and mix thoroughly with remaining brownie ingredients. Pour into a buttered 8-inch square pan. Bake for 30 minutes. Cool in pan. Cut brownies into squares.

Icing: Mix all ingredients in saucepan and bring to a boil, stirring constantly. Simmer 1 minute and remove from heat. When cooled a bit, add Kahlua. Spread icing over brownies and sprinkle with chocolate chips or chocolate shavings for garnish.

Key Lime Pie

Makes 6-8 servings

4	large eggs yolks	1	teaspoon vanilla
1	can sweetened condensed milk	1	9-inch graham cracker pie crust
½	cup key lime juice, fresh or bottled		

Meringue:

4	egg whites	½	cup sugar, approximately

Preheat oven 350°.

In medium mixing bowl, beat egg yolks until pale and ribbon-like. Slowly add sweetened condensed milk, beat until well blended.

Slowly add key lime juice, and then the vanilla. Pour into graham cracker crust. Bake for 10 minutes. Remove from oven.

Increase oven to broil, place baking rack closest to top. Make meringue: In clean mixing bowl place egg whites, beat until beginning to froth, then add 2 tablespoons of sugar at a time until the mixture is stiff and smooth, you may not need all the sugar. Spread the meringue on top of pie, sealing at the edges. Place under broiler for 2 to 3 minutes or until browned. BE VERY CAREFUL and watch this ... it can burn quickly. Cool before serving.

Maple Walnut Cranberry Pie

Makes 6-8 servings

1	9-inch pie crust chilled, but not frozen	¼	teaspoon salt
¼	cup butter	1	cup walnuts, coarsely chopped
¾	cup sugar	1	cup cranberries, coarsely chopped
4	large eggs	8	whole walnuts, for garnish
¾	cup light corn syrup		whipped cream or ice cream, for garnish
¼	cup maple syrup		
1	teaspoon vanilla		
1	teaspoon cinnamon		

Preheat oven 375°. Place oven rack in lower third of oven.

In large mixing bowl, cream butter, add sugar and cream again. Add eggs, one at a time. Add corn syrup, maple syrup, vanilla, cinnamon and salt. Beat until smooth.

Fold in nuts and cranberries, pour into well chilled pie crust and garnish with whole walnuts as desired.

Bake 40 to 45 minutes, or until pie sets and no longer jiggles.

Cool completely and serve with whipped cream or ice cream.

One-Pan Chocolate Coffee Cake

Makes 6 servings

2½	cups all-purpose flour	2	tablespoons cider vinegar
1½	cups sugar	⅔	cup vegetable oil
½	cup cocoa	2	cups cold coffee (or water)
2	teaspoons baking soda	⅓	cup sugar
½	teaspoon salt	1	teaspoon cinnamon
1	tablespoon vanilla		

Preheat oven to 350°.

Stir together flour, 1½ cups sugar, cocoa, baking soda, and salt in an ungreased 12-inch by 8-inch baking pan. Make 3 wells in the mixture; pour vanilla in the first well, pour vinegar in the second and oil in the remaining well. Pour in coffee and stir all with a fork until well mixed. Spread mixture in an even layer. Combine remaining ⅓ cup sugar with the cinnamon, sprinkle ½ of this over batter. Bake 35 to 40 minutes or when toothpick inserted comes out clean. Remove from oven and sprinkle remaining sugar/cinnamon over hot cake. Cool 15 minutes before cutting.

Pumpkin Pie

Makes 6–8 servings

1	9-inch deep dish fresh or frozen pie crust	1	teaspoon ground cinnamon
2	large eggs, slightly beaten	½	teaspoon ground allspice
1	can pumpkin, solid pack	½	teaspoon ginger
¾	cup sugar	1⅔	cups half and half
½	teaspoon salt	¼	cup pecans, chopped, optional

Preheat oven to 375°. Let pie crust thaw, if frozen. Combine ingredients in above order, blending well. Pour into pie crust. Bake 1 hour to 1¼ hours on a cookie sheet, or until center tests done. Serve with whipped cream or ice cream.

Sweet Potato Crumb Pie

Makes 6–8 servings

1	9-inch fresh or frozen pie crust	½	cup butter, melted
3	cups sweet potato, cooked and mashed	1	cup light brown sugar, packed
½	cup sugar	¼	cup flour
2	large eggs, beaten	1	teaspoon allspice
¼	cup Jack Daniels Tennessee Whiskey	1	teaspoon cinnamon
⅓	cup half and half	1	cup pecans, chopped
		¼	cup butter, melted

Preheat oven to 375°. Let pie crust thaw, if frozen. Combine sweet potatoes, sugar, eggs, whiskey, half and half, and butter. Spread into pie crust. Combine remaining ingredients and spread over pie, like a crust. Bake 25 to 30 minutes or until center tests done. If edges of crust begin to get too brown, wrap edges with foil and continue to bake. Let cool to set before slicing.

Traditional King Cake

Makes 10 servings

½ cup warm water (110° to 115°)

2 packages active dry yeast

½ cup plus 1 teaspoon sugar

3½ to 4½ cups unsifted flour

1 teaspoon nutmeg

2 teaspoons salt

1 teaspoon lemon zest

5 egg yolks

½ cup warm whole milk

1 stick butter, cut into slices and softened

2 tablespoons butter, softened for greasing

1 teaspoon cinnamon

1 egg, slightly beaten with 1 tablespoon milk

1 to 2-inch baby doll charm

Icing:

3 cups confectioner's sugar

1 to 4 cups lemon juice

3 to 4 tablespoons water

Garnish:
  yellow, purple and green sugar sprinkles

This cake is a Mardi Gras tradition and goes well with many Cajun dishes. Whoever gets the baby doll gets good luck for the rest of the year!

Pour warm water into a small bowl, and sprinkle yeast and 1 teaspoon sugar into it. Let yeast and sugar rest 3 minutes, then mix thoroughly. Set bowl in a warm place for 10 minutes, or until yeast bubbles. In a large bowl, sift together 3½ cups of flour, remaining sugar, nutmeg and salt. Stir in lemon zest. Make well in center of dry ingredients; add yeast mixture and warm milk. Add egg yolks using a wooden spoon, slowly combining wet ingredients with dry. When mixture is smooth, beat in stick of softened butter, 1 tablespoon at a time and continue to beat 2

(Continued on next page)

Traditional King Cake *(Continued from previous page)*

minutes or until dough can be formed into a medium soft ball. Place dough on lightly floured surface and knead, adding up to 1 more cup of flour, 1 tablespoon at a time. When dough is no longer sticky, knead 10 minutes until shiny and elastic. Coat the inside of a large bowl with softened butter. Place dough ball in bowl and rotate until the entire surface is buttered. Cover bowl with kitchen towel, or plastic wrap, and set in draft-free spot for about 1½ hours, or until it doubles in volume. Coat a large baking sheet with butter. Remove dough from bowl and place on lightly floured surface. Using fist, punch down dough with a heavy blow. Sprinkle cinnamon over the top, pat and shape the dough into a cylinder. Twist dough to form a curled cylinder and place on buttered baking sheet, pinching the ends to close the circle. Cover dough with towel or plastic wrap and set in a draft-free spot for about 45 minutes, or until double in volume. Preheat oven to 375°. Brush top and sides of cake with egg wash and bake on middle rack of oven for 25 to 35 minutes or until golden brown. Place on wire rack to cool. Push baby doll charm inside cake to hide it. Mix together icing ingredients and ice the cake. Sprinkle top of cake with purple, green and yellow sugar crystals. Cake is generally served in large 2-inch to 3-inch slices.

Triple Chocolate Brownie Pie

Makes 6 – 8 servings

2	eggs	½	cup semi-sweet chocolate chips
1	cup sugar	½	cup pecans or walnuts, chopped
½	cup butter, melted	1	teaspoon vanilla extract
½	cup all-purpose flour		ice cream
⅓	cup cocoa		chocolate syrup, heated
¼	teaspoon salt		

Preheat oven to 350°. Grease 9-inch pie plate. In small bowl, beat eggs blend in sugar and butter. In separate bowl, stir together flour, cocoa and salt; add egg mixture, beating until blended. Stir in chocolate chips, nuts and vanilla. Spread batter into prepared pie plate. Bake 35 minutes or until set, pie will still be moist in center. Cool completely, cut into wedges, serve with ice cream and top with warmed chocolate syrup.

White Chocolate Amaretto Crème Brûlée

Makes 4 servings

4	large egg yolks	¼	pound white chocolate, shaved or grated
3	tablespoons sugar		
1	cup heavy cream	2	tablespoons Amaretto liqueur
1	cup half and half		additional sugar for topping

Preheat oven to 300°. Prepare a bain-marie ... a baking dish with water. Whisk egg yolks and sugar together. In a medium saucepan, bring heavy cream and half and half to a boil. Reduce heat to low and add chocolate, stirring to melt. Remove from heat and add egg mixture, a little at a time until blended; add Amaretto. Pour mixture into 4 custard cups and place in baking pan with water that comes half-way up the sides of the custard cups. Bake 50 minutes or until set in the middle. Remove from bain marie. Sprinkle with thin layer of sugar and place under broiler or torch with a torch gun to form a caramelized top.

Nutritional Information

In today's world of watching fat grams, game meats and birds are generally lower in fat and cholesterol than many domestic meats and poultry. For home cooks and chefs wild game is a wonderful alternative in low-fat diets. This chart compares nutrition among one serving portions, approximately 4 oz. raw portions.

Large Game	Calories	Fat (g)	% Fat/Cal.	Cholesterol (mg)
Antelope (pronghorn)	114	2	17	95
Bear	161	8	48	no data
Beef, hamburger, lean*	272	18	63	87
Beefalo, all cuts	143	5	32	44
Boar	122	3	26	no data
Buffalo, American	109	2	16	62
Caribou	127	3	25	83
Deer	120	2	19	85
Elk	111	1	12	55
oat, domestic	109	2	20	57
Moose	102	0.7	7	59
Venison	124	2	14	no data
Venison, dried, salted	142	1	6	no data

Small/Exotic Game	Calories	Fat (g)	% Fat/Cal.	Cholesterol (mg)
Alligator	148	3	18	65
Armadillo	174	7	38	73
Beaver	146	5	31	no data
Frog legs, floured, fried	290	20	63	no data
Hare (jack rabbit)	153	3	20	131
Kangaroo	93	0.5	2	62
Muskrat	162	8	47	no data
Opossum	188	9	43	no data
Rabbit, domestic	136	6	38	57
Rabbit, wild (cottontail)	144	2	20	77
Raccoon	217	12	53	no data
Squirrel	120	3	25	83
Turtle	89	0.5	5	50

*For purposes of comparison.

Sources of information included the U.S. Department of Agriculture and Ms. Downen with the University of Tennessee Agriculture Department.

Nutritional Information

Birds	Calories	Fat (g)	% Fat/Cal.	Cholesterol (mg)
Chicken, domestic, breast, no skin*	165	4	21	81
Chicken, domestic, dark meat, with skin*	237	18	71	82
Chicken, domestic, thigh, no skin*	119	4	31	83
Dove, domestic, with skin	151	2	15	91
Duck, domestic, with skin	404	39	88	76
Duckling, farm-raised, breast, no skin	132	2	14	153
Duckling, farm-raised, breast, with skin	193	11	51	135
Duckling, farm-raised, leg, no skin	163	5	28	117
Duckling, farm-raised, leg, with skin	206	11	48	113
Duck, wild, breast, no skin	123	4	32	no data
Duck, wild, breast, with skin	211	15	66	80
Duck, wild, mallard	154	2	16	143
Emu, farm-raised, no skin	120	3	23	45
Goose, domestic, no skin	161	7	41	84
Goose, domestic, with skin	371	34	83	80
Goose, wild, Canadian	171	4	28	105
Grouse, wild, sharp-tailed	142	1	6	106
Guinea hen, with skin	156	6	38	53
Ostrich, farm-raised, no skin	107	2	15	61
Pheasant, farm-raised, with skin	151	5	33	49
Pheasant, wild, breast, no skin	134	3	26	49
Pheasant, wild, with skin	181	9	48	no data
Poussin, farm-raised, with skin	166	11	61	51
Quail breast, wild, no skin	123	3	23	no data
Quail, whole, wild, with skin	193	12	58	no data
Squab (pigeon), farm-raised, breast, no skin	144	8	49	no data
Squab (pigeon), farm raised, with skin	297	24	74	no data
Turkey breast, domestic, with skin	167	8	46	62
Turkey leg, domestic, dark, no skin	187	7	36	85
Turkey, domestic, light/dark, no skin	170	5	28	76
Turkey, domestic, light, no skin	114	2	13	62

*For purposes of comparison.

Sources of information included the U.S. Department of Agriculture and Ms. Downen with the University of Tennessee Agriculture Department.

ORDER FORM
Flavorful Wild Game

ORDER:

_____ copies of Flavorful Wild Game @ $21.95 each $_____

Shipping and handling per book @ $3.40 each $_____

Tennessee residents add 9.25% sales tax $_____

Total $_____

PAYMENT METHOD:

☐ Check, enclosed is my check or money order, made payable to:

Chef Valerie, LLC

Credit Card: ☐ M/C Visa   ☐ Amex   ☐ Discover

Card Number_____ Exp. Date: _____

Signature:_____

SHIP TO:

Name:_____

Address:_____

City: _____ State: _____ Zip:_____

Telephone: _____

E-mail address (for notification):_____

Personalization: _____

MAIL TO:
Chef Valerie
1163 River Oaks View Cove
Memphis, TN 38120

Please allow 4 to 6 weeks for delivery.
OR Order Online at
www.chefval.com